CO-003

A COMPLETE INTRODUCTION TO

SETTING UP AN AQUARIUM

Livebearers are among the most popular of aquarium fishes, and the exquisite shape and color of this Red Lyretail Swordtail testify to the beauty of many cultivated strains. Photo by E. C. Taylor.

Aquarium keeping is a family hobby. It appeals to all members of the family. Over 20,000,000 people in the U.S. keep fishes; England boasts 11,000,000 while Australia and Canada claim 1,000,000 hobbyists each. Specialized aquarium stores sell everything necessary for a successful aquarium.

A COMPLETE INTRODUCTION TO

SETTING UP AN AQUARIUM

COMPLETELY ILLUSTRATED IN FULL COLOR

A beautiful community aquarium full of Tetras and Swordtails. Photo by B. Kahl.

Jim Kelly

1995 Edition

Distributed in the UNITED STATES to the Pet Trade by T.F.H. Publications, Inc., One T.F.H. Plaza, Neptune City, NJ 07753; distributed in the UNITED STATES to the Bookstore and Library Trade by National Book Network, Inc. 4720 Boston Way, Lanham MD 20706; in CANADA to the Pet Trade by H & L Pet Supplies Inc., 27 Kingston Crescent, Kitchener, Ontario N2B 2T6; Rolf C. Hagen Ltd., 3225 Sartelon Street, Montreal 382 Quebec; in CANADA to the Book Trade by Vanwell Publishing Ltd., 1 Northrup Crescent, St. Catharines, Ontario L2M 6P5 ; in ENGLAND by T.F.H. Publications, PO Box 15, Waterlooville PO7 6BQ; in AUSTRALIA AND THE SOUTH PACIFIC by T.F.H. (Australia), Pty. Ltd., Box 149, Brookvale 2100 N.S.W., Australia; in NEW ZEALAND by Brooklands Aquarium Ltd. 5 McGiven Drive, New Plymouth, RD1 New Zealand; in Japan by T.F.H. Publications, Japan—Jiro Tsuda, 10-12-3 Ohjidai, Sakura, Chiba 285, Japan; in SOUTH AFRICA by Lopis (Pty) Ltd., P.O. Box 39127, Booysens, 2016, Johannesburg, South Africa. Published by T.F.H. Publications, Inc.
MANUFACTURED IN THE UNITED STATES OF AMERICA
BY T.F.H. PUBLICATIONS, INC.

Contents

A Short History of Aquarium Keeping

Those who cannot remember the past are condemned to repeat it!
These words of wisdom are to be found emblazoned on the wall of the Aeronautical Museum, Terminal Building, at the John F. Kennedy International Airport, New York. It is a reply to those people who might ask why a book such as this should contain a history of fish and the story of the men who kept and observed them.

Keeping fish in captivity is an ancient art, though how ancient, we shall probably never know. However, records show that in

The keeping of aquaria has been popular for centuries. Some of the older designs are considered antiques and are highly prized by collectors. Although today's aquaria are certainly more functional, they are not nearly as ornate!

early China — long before the birth of Christ — the keeping and breeding of Carp was a flourishing business. In fact *The Book of Vermilion Fish* is credited to Chang Chi'en-te, a Chinese author who lived more than one thousand years before our present western calendar began.

The Greeks seem to have had a word for everything, so it is no surprise that Aristotle (384-322 BC), called "The Father of All Learning," set down and described many species of fishes brought to him. Lacking the benefits of Carl Linnaeus' principles for defining genera and species, he used common names — common, that is, to the fishermen of the Aegean Sea. Perhaps it was a good thing that their numbers were limited to just over one hundred species!

Then for hundreds of years, men gave the subject little

thought. They merely parroted the Aristotelian teachings, adding little to our knowledge. Archeologists have uncovered evidence that the Romans kept fish in containers. However, I suspect that the Romans were more interested in enhancing the pleasures of their cuisine than in contributing to science.

A modern book about life under the Egyptian kings quotes the following:

In the gardens at the Palace of Tutmosis the Third, were to be found huge ornamental tanks containing fish; they served the dual purpose of decoration and as a means of keeping down the mosquitos.

Across the ocean in the New World, the Spanish invaders under Cortez were searching for the gold in "El Dorado." They found plenty of "gold" fish in the

Goldfish have been bred for over a thousand years, and are an important feature of Oriental art and culture.

varied collection of fish and fowl in the gardens of the Montezuman prince, a collection that he had inherited!

The common goldfish (according to Duerigen) reached Europe about 1611 — the time Henry Hudson was embarking upon his last voyage. When the city of London burned in the Great Fire of 1666, the famous diarist Samuel Pepys was filling the pages of his journal with a description of "fishes kept in a glass of water"; across the English Channel in Strasbourg, Leonhart Baldner was acting like a Nero of the Middle Ages by passing his time "fiddling" with fish kept in glass containers.

The Basic Requirements

Obviously, the first piece of equipment required is a fish tank.

Choosing a tank is similar to buying a new automobile — which one would suit your taste and fill your requirements is a very individual matter. The Chinese had a saying, "One picture is worth a thousand words," and a little time spent viewing the tanks and stands available in your local tank filled with water, gravel and rock weighs about 100 pounds. Sorry, but that beautiful ornate coffee table just won't do unless you want a "disaster area" in your home! Tanks with stand setups are worthy of consideration and allow you greater freedom of choice when planning a location for the aquarium.

Cuboid tanks are the shape most commonly seen used for aquariums, but tanks in the form of other regular polygons, such as hexagons and octagons, also are available. California Aquarium Supply Co.

pet store will be more valuable than a whole chapter on the subject. The following suggestions are to guide you in making a final decision.

Unless you already have a substantial base on which to place your tank, you will require a stand. The average ten-gallon

Often, beginners automatically choose a small tank. This is not advisable, as it is easier to maintain a large aquarium than a small one.

Choose a size (bearing in mind the surface area) that gives a nice, deep front view. Around 10 to 20 gallons capacity should be about right.

If you do not contemplate a manufactured reflector (tank cover/light holder), then cover the top with a piece of glass. This will help to keep out dust and will stop your prize fish from committing hari-kari by leaping out onto the carpet. Glass covers will not restrict the air supply.

The glass in your aquarium is held in place by special cement and, though strong, won't stand knocking about. Carry your

Fluorescent tubes for aquarium lighting fixtures come in a number of different wattages and spectra. Pet dealers can provide practical advice about which type of tube is best for a particular tank setup. Photo courtesy of Coralife/Energy Savers.

container home as if it were some rare piece of Dresden china. If you put your tank on a piece of furniture, place it on a pad of felt or plastic to prevent furniture damage.

Lighting the Aquarium

Ever since the pronouncement in the Book of Genesis, "Let there be light!" fishkeepers have been hotly debating what sort of light to use. If your original purchase was a package deal, it probably included a reflector to house the lights. Reflectors manufactured today are well-made, rugged, and safe, and add a professional

finish to one's set-up.

In their natural environment, fishes receive light from above, so do not experiment by lighting your tank from the sides or below.

The amount of wattage needed will vary, but your pet dealer will advise you. A good formula for calculating the amount of wattage is:

$$\text{Wattage required} = \frac{\text{Length of tank in inches} \times 32}{\text{Number of hours the tank is lit}}$$

From experience, I recommend fluorescent lighting, but I choose the color of the tube carefully. Experiments carried out by leading authorities prove that fishes do better under this type of lighting when the color tends towards the reds and yellows; under blue light some fish stop breeding. Blue light adversely affects fish eggs!

Reflectors serve useful purposes apart from being just lampholders.

Filters

Talk fish with any old-timer and he will tell you that to succeed in the "good old days" of the hobby, without the modern advantages of filtration, you *had* to be good. In fact, some of these senior aquarists still insist that filters are unnecessary, but so many aquarists have proved the worth of filtration that it is here to stay.

That it is possible to run a successful aquarium without the use of filters or aeration cannot be denied, but just ask the lady of the house whether she would prefer to go back to the old-fashioned broom instead of her vacuum cleaner, and you have your answer. Anything that helps to cut down on the work and make the hobby more pleasurable is obviously an advantage of which one should make full use. What, then, is the function of filtration?

a) It helps to keep the water clean and give it that "good enough to drink" appearance by removing the floating debris.
b) It circulates the water in the tank, insuring a better exchange of gases and a better distribution of air.
c) By passing the water through media like activated charcoal, harmful waste products are removed. Bear in mind that no filter will remove waste products *dissolved* in the water; regular replacement by a partial change of the tank water is desirable even when filtration is employed.

Filter systems are many and varied. The more conventional ones usually take the form of plastic boxes hung outside or inside the tank and contain filter material such as polyester floss or sponge. To facilitate the movement of water from the aquarium through the "sieve" and back again to the tank, they utilize an air lift and a siphon. The action of these conventional filters is largely mechanical and they are designed primarily to remove the particulate materials from the water.

There are also a number of excellent power filters on the market. These utilize a motor to pull or drive water through the filter media which are contained in a box or cylinder outside the tank. Most of these function both mechanically and biologically, filtering large volumes of water very efficiently. Most have a powerful return flow that aerates very efficiently.

Another type of filter fits underneath the aquarium gravel, and the action of breaking down the particulate material into gases (CO_2) and soluble nitrates is biological. That is, this type of filter circulates oxygen-rich water through the gravel. The oxygen encourages the growth of beneficial bacteria that break down the organic matter in the tank and thus helps to prevent pollution. This biological action is also present to a lesser extent in the conventional types. Remember, efficient as these filters are in removing debris from the water, they will not remove certain natural acids, oils or detergents.

There are filters which can remove particles of colloidal size (substances which, though apparently dissolved, cannot pass through a membrane, such as bacteria, certain types of algae and protozoa). These are the so-called "water polishers," which utilize diatomaceous earth as a filter medium.

No one filter system is perfect and each must be used correctly if maximum efficiency and

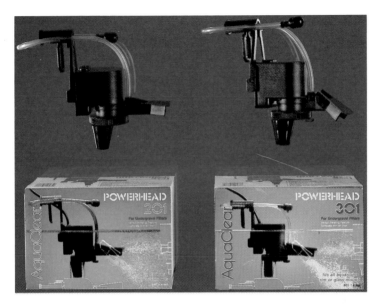

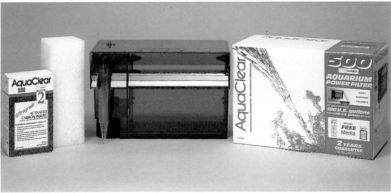

Upper photo: *power heads can be attached to undergravel filters to increase flow rate and biological filtration activity or can be used alone to provide added aeration and water movement.* **Lower photo:** *Power filters come in many different forms, but all are relatively much more effective than the older style air-operated filters. Both photos courtesy of Hagen.*

utilization is to be achieved by the hobbyist. Your choice will largely depend on the funds available and the job you want it to do. Describe your aquarium to your dealer and seek his experience in these matters.

If you choose one of the conventional types that use filter media, remember that you must change or clean this frequently if the filter is to function properly. Some man-made filter materials can be rinsed under a faucet and be reused.

Also available and very useful

Plants are often used to "soften" the edges of rocks or driftwood.

adjuncts to one's filter cleaning kit are long, flexible brushes. These filter brushes come in various sizes and are used to clean around the twists and bends of the plastic piping.

Aeration

Aeration consists of agitating the water by means of a stream of air forced through a porous medium such as an airstone. For best results, the stream of air bubbles should be neither fine nor coarse. After prolonged usage, the pores of the stone can become clogged. A few minutes' immersion in vinegar and a brisk rub with a stiff brush will restore its porosity. Various ceramic aerator ornaments are available as substitutes for air stones, or you can have multiple sources of air bubbling in your tank by the use of a series of air valves. These can be made of metal or plastic, and can vary from a simple T-shaped pipe to more complicated affairs sporting an air control,

screw valve, or other device.

Before connecting the aerator to the pump, blow gently down the tubing. There should be a free flow of air through the aerator. If effort is required, then re-check the tubing and the stones for blockage. If you regularly examine your system in this way, you will lengthen the life of your air pump.

Air tubing carries the air from the pump to the various parts of your filtration or aeration system. Manufactured from clear or colored plastic, the choice lies mainly in personal preference. If you want the tubing to be inconspicuous, then use a clear plastic, though this has a tendency to kink and harden when old.

Various clamps, either metal or plastic, are often attached onto tubing to regulate the amount of air passing through.

Heaters and Thermostats

Before discussing how to keep fishes in the proper water temperature, let us examine the scales used to measure temperature. Too many writers assume that their readers "must know about that!" I have more respect for my readers than to take them for granted.

Three systems exist to measure temperature. The first (abbreviated F), propounded by Gabriel Fahrenheit and bearing his name, registers the freezing point of water at 32°F and the boiling point at 212°F. The second method, named after a Swedish scientist, Anders Celsius, registers the freezing point of water at 0°C and the boiling point at 100°C. The latter measure, usually called Centigrade (abbreviated C), is used by scientists and in countries utilizing the metric system. Fahrenheit is popular in the United States and Great Britain, and we shall use F° temperatures unless otherwise indicated. The third system, the Kelvin scale, is a metric scale used in laboratories.

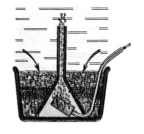

To meet the temperature requirements of each fish likely to find its way into our aquariums, our tank water would have to range between 65° and 85°F. It is best to aim for a happy medium, which experience suggests is about 75°F. Do not become a "thermometer worshipper," panicking if the thermometer registers slightly above or below 75°F. Fishes are amazingly adaptable and can withstand a gradual change of temperature provided it doesn't cover too great a range. Even a change of five degrees during the night will cause no harm, so do not worry over a thermometer reading anywhere from 73° to 78°.

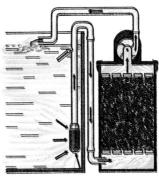

*Three types of filters. **Top:** Air-driven sponge filter. **Center:** Gravel filter. **Bottom:** Motor-driven canister filter.*

Thermometers come in various shapes and sizes. Cheaper ones have their column filled with colored alcohol; the better ones use mercury, and some have a purely mechanical mechanism. Though the thermometer can be hidden away in the aquarium, it is usual to fasten it to the inside of the front glass. In this position a reading can be taken quickly and easily. Whatever sort of thermometer you purchase, have its accuracy checked first. Heat-

A heating unit consists of a coil of wire that becomes hot when a current of electricity is passed through it. The wire is protected and waterproofed by being enclosed in a glass tube. If the heater were allowed to heat continuously, the water in the tank would soon become too hot for our fishes, so an automatic switch control is incorporated in the circuit — we call this switch a "thermostat."

Briefly, a thermostat is a switch

The two most popular styles of aquarium heater are the completely submergible style and the hanging style. Submergible heaters are intended to be completely immersed in the water, usually at the bottom of the tank, whereas hanging heaters sit on the rim of the tank and must be only partially submerged. Both types are available in a wide range of wattages. Heaters shown are of the submergible type. Photo courtesy of Hagen.

sensitive color strips are also available.

Having agreed that the water in our tank must be kept at a fairly regular temperature, we now turn to the various ways of achieving this. In the past, gas and oil were employed but were messy and cumbersome. They filled the gap until the coming of electricity made things much simpler and cleaner.

consisting of two strips of metal welded together, each having a different *coefficient of expansion*. This bi-metallic strip expands when heated. As one piece of metal expands more than the other, the strip curves and in bending acts as a make-and-break switch. To avoid interference with radio and TV, a radio condenser is provided.

Though both heater and thermostat can be purchased as separate units, they are better combined into one. This is usually hidden away by hanging it from the rear top edge of the aquarium. All units contain a small neon indicator light — a visible reminder that all is well.

For the heater size required, discuss the size of your tank with your dealer and let him advise the proper wattage. An approximate guide is to multiply the gallon capacity of the tank by five. For example, a 25 watt heater for a five gallon tank, 50 watts for a

Safety is also due to the high standards now set by the manufacturers. Make sure all connections are safe, and if you don't understand electricity, get someone who does to do the job.

Gravel

As soil is to your garden, so gravel is to your aquarium. A good thick layer is needed to cover the floor of the tank, not only for decorative purposes but also to provide a rooting medium

With some hood designs, a pane of glass separates the hood from the tank itself.

ten, and so on.

Thermostats are pre-set by the maker at around 75°F. Most have a small adjustment screw to adjust the setting. Don't play around with this adjustment more than is absolutely necessary. If you do have occasion to remove this piece of equipment from the water, *be sure to disconnect the power first.* The combination of electricity and water is like James Bond — licensed to kill! With proper use, accidents are rare.

for your plants. Collecting your own gravel is not worth the risk of introducing parasites and infection. Gravel is usually cheap and can be bought in an assortment of colors to suit your taste. One pound covers an area of roughly 20 cubic inches, but if you are going to "landscape" your aquarium, it is better to have too much than too little. The actual area covered varies with the composition of the gravel and its mesh size. The gravel grains should be from two to three times the size of a pin head. Too fine a gravel, or sand packed too tightly, inhibits the circulation of water; too coarse a gravel allows particles of food to lodge in between — out of the reach of fishes and cleaning devices. This uneaten food can become a focal point for pollution.

Pumps

These are necessary to provide

In a typical corner filter, a flow of air pulls water through the filter media .

air for your filtration and aeration equipment. Though the cost will be a consideration when making your choice, get the best you can afford. Many beginners purchase a small-output pump, sufficient only for their early requirements. Before long, they find that they need more air and either buy another small motor, or, as is usually the case, a larger model. Buying a more powerful pump at the start is both sensible and economical.

Pumps fall into two main categories: the vibrator, which relies on a make-and-break circuit to operate a diaphragm (similar to the circuitry used in an electric door bell), and the piston pump, which, as its name suggests, makes use of the air provided by a pumping action of a piston and cylinder. Some vibrators are apt to be low in output and noisy. What didn't sound loud in the hubbub of the store can drive you to distraction in the quiet of a room at home.

All types of pumps consume very little current and come complete, ready to connect. Some makes of pump, when stopped, allow the water in the tank to siphon back down the air tubing, which can ruin the pump mechanism, blow the electric fuses, and cause a mess on the floor! Play safe. Fit a check valve in the air tube between pump and tank or, better still, place the motor higher than the tank. Some manufacturers design their models to be hung from the rear wall of the aquarium. Follow the maker's recommendations regarding servicing, particularly for oiling. The more expensive "motor" type pumps include a bottle of special vegetable (non-toxic) oil for this purpose. Vibrator pumps ordinarily require little servicing.

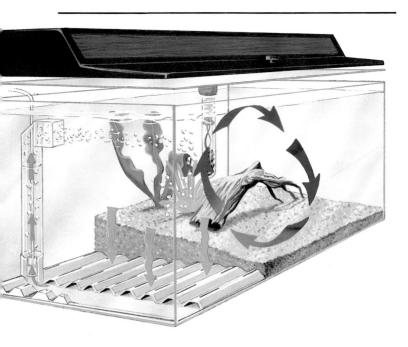

Top: *This diagram illustrates how an undergravel filter functions. Water is drawn down through the gravel bed, where it is biologically filtered, and is returned via the corner lift tubes. In addition, the flow from the lift tubes circulates the water effectively.*

Vibrator air pumps are available in a number of different sizes and air output capacities to suit differing tank and equipment requirements. Photo courtesy of Hagen.

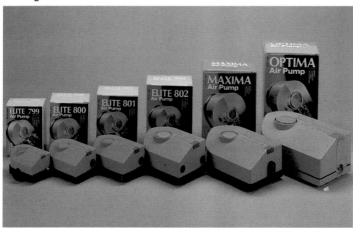

Making a Start

Now that you are in possession of the ingredients for setting up a tropical aquarium, you will no doubt be anxious to make a start.

Success comes before work only in the dictionary; for your aquarium to be a credit you must work. In reading this book you have already shown your willingness to learn the correct way of doing things, so don't spoil

little patience and forethought now can save hours of trouble in the future.

A Site for the Tank

The decision as to where to place the aquarium will obviously rest with you. But if the stand is placed near a wall, leave sufficient room to hang a box filter on the back of the tank as

When well set up and maintained, an aquarium is more than a fish tank–it is an attractive piece of furniture.

your efforts at this stage by being over-anxious.

Despite the desires of the family to see the aquarium in operation, you must resist the temptation to skimp on the preparations. To have a crystal-clear tank in the future, it must be carefully set up in the beginning. Too few aquarists realize that a

well as enough space to enable you to reach any electrical connections hanging there.

The next step is to insure that the tank and stand are perfectly level. If they are not, the water in the tank will be lopsided, and as a filled aquarium is enormously heavy and difficult to adjust, level it while it's empty.

And make no attempt to move the aquarium once it is filled with water (in the case of the large tanks, I doubt whether you could), but do give the site some careful thought.

Cover the immediate floor area with newspapers or, better still, the large plastic bags from the cleaners. This will protect the carpet and the floor.

Now that we've taken care of the preliminaries, let's examine the tank. Clean it inside and out with salt and water, being careful not to use anything that will scratch the glass. Use no fluid detergents or soaps of any kind. Then rinse and wipe. Any small pieces of cement left by the manufacturer can be scraped off with a razor blade but don't trim too much; otherwise, on filling, you might find a leaking tank.

Washing the Gravel

Gravel may appear clean enough when you make your purchase but before new gravel can be placed in the tank it must be rinsed thoroughly under a swift flowing jet of water. Clean a small portion at a time and stir the gravel in a bucket continuously until the water flowing off is running clean. Only then is the gravel ready for the aquarium.

Shallow gravel not only looks wrong, it doesn't provide a deep enough bed for the plant roots. It's cheap, so spread it thick. Rocks can be used to hold it together in pockets and if the rocks are left slightly protruding above the surface of the gravel they will appear more natural looking. Use about two pounds of gravel for each gallon of water. Extremely high tanks may require less.

Experience has shown that advice to slope the stones from the rear of the tank to the front is

Aquarium substrates come in many different forms, with gravel and glass being among the most popular. Both gravels and glasses are available in different grit sizes and a wide range of colors; they also can be selected for varying degrees of jaggedness.

21

reaction between small amounts of iron in the stones and hydrogen sulphide produced by anaerobic bacteria. If you feed the fish more food than they can eat, surplus food will drop to the bottom, where it will decay, causing an oxygen deficiency and pollution of the water. The first signs of this appear when the gravel starts to go black. If the process goes too far, then you have no alternative but to break everything down and start afresh.

Reminder: do not use soaps or detergents when cleaning tank or gravel!

Products designed to make the cultivation of living aquarium plants much easier than it would be without their stabilizing and nutritive influences are available and easy to use. Photo courtesy of Aquarium Products.

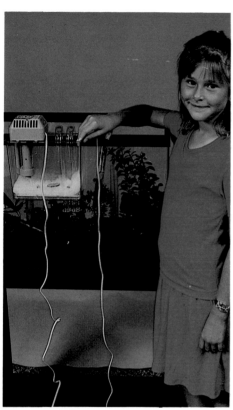

Even the setting up of an aquarium can be fun! Photo by Dr. Herbert R. Axelrod.

a waste of time. After the aquarium is established the movement of both fish and water will level out the substrate. This doesn't mean that the floor has to be flat and uninspiring; careful use of rock will hold the gravel together and help undulate the surface. Try to emulate a natural contour to add character to the scene.

With all the gravel and rock in place, take a good close look at it. See how nice and clean it looks? Well, aim to keep it just like that in the future! Blackening of aquarium gravel is due to the

Artificial plants can be purchased in a variety of sizes, which allows aquarists to create attractive waterscapes by placing small plants in the foreground, grading to larger plants toward the rear of the tank. Photo courtesy of Hagen.

Plants

Start by rinsing the plants you have purchased under a lukewarm tap. Subjecting plants to cold water only sets them back, and they take time to recover. Examine each plant for snails and any other small pests which often adhere to the stems and leaves. A quick dip in a strong salt solution usually makes them release their hold on the plant.

After sorting the plants into groups according to size, fill the tank halfway with lukewarm water

Numerous artificial decorations are available to adorn your tanks, including intricate plastic caves and rockworks that provide shelter as well as decoration. Photo courtesy of Blue Ribbon Pet Products.

from a clean bucket. Pour the water gently so that the main flow is directed onto a saucer placed inside the aquarium, resting on the surface of the stones. If done this way the filling won't disturb the gravel. Though this isn't as important at this stage as the final filling, there is no point in breaking down what you have just built up.

Planting in shallow water is much simpler than planting dry; the water allows the leaves to rise and spread, giving a better idea of just how your decorative scheme is progressing. Start planting at the back and work your way forward. If you have to break off

this operation, the water in the tank will prevent the plants from drying out, but in that event cover the unplanted plants with wet newspaper.

Planting: hold each plant firmly at the crown. This is located at the junction where the roots join the stem or main body. With one finger make a path in the gravel and slide the roots into this. On no account try to force the roots down or you will just break them off. Bury the roots and stem as deeply as possible; then, when in position, grasp all the stems together and gently tug upwards until the crown is just visible. When planting bunches be sure not to disturb any already set in place.

Bunch plants come fastened together with strips of lead, wire, string, raffia or even rubber bands, without roots. You should bury the base of the clump just below the gravel; most of these will develop root growths later. If the bunch tends to float, weight it down by either sprinkling gravel among the leaves or fastening the clump firmly with small pieces of lead. Though this metal in strip form isn't toxic in the aquarium, bunches so fastened tend to rot where the plant comes into contact with the metal.

Set all but the floating plants in place. These are not placed on the surface of the water until after the aquarium is filled. Float them temporarily in a container of lukewarm water and they will come to no harm.

Installing the Equipment

With all the plants in place and the tank still half full of water, the heater/thermostat can now be affixed to the back of the frame. If placed near one end it can be easily camouflaged by the taller plants.

To function correctly the heater must be immersed in the water (when the aquarium is filled) for approximately three-quarters of its length, but all manufacturers of this equipment include some form of fixing clip or bracket. *Do not connect to the power at this stage.*

If filters and/or aerators are to be used, it is also time to install them. In the case of box filter units, see that they are complete with filter media. If this includes

Most heaters clamp onto the plastic rim of the tank. Photos by Dr. Herbert R. Axelrod.

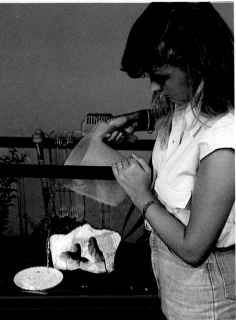

charcoal, rinse by placing the charcoal in a coarse net and swirling it under a faucet. Charcoal sold in packets contains quite a lot of loose dust and this must be rinsed out before putting the charcoal into the filter box.

Appliances come boxed with full installation instructions; follow these recommendations and you can't go wrong. If the water is delivered to the filter by a siphon, it cannot be started until after the tank is completely filled.

Electrical Connections

The average aquarium requires power outlets for the heater, the reflector (lights), and the air pump or power filter.

Aquarium appliances consume very little electricity and they come ready-wired, complete with a two-pronged plug. All you have to do is connect them to a power outlet. Don't drape wiring all over the tank as though you were decorating a Christmas tree. Loose, dangling wire is both dangerous and unsightly. Use tape to fasten it out of sight. But should the length of the wire supplied not be long enough, it is easier to fit a 3-outlet plug near the tank and run a single extension to the supply than to extend all the other wiring.

Filling the Tank

When all is in place — with the power still not connected — give the inside glass a final rinse and wipe away any scum that might have accrued from the previous operations. Siphon out the water you used to simplify planting, as it will no doubt be dirty. Give the

After all decorations are placed in the aquarium, it is filled with water, taking care not to overly disturb the gravel. Photos by Dr. Herbert R. Axelrod.

inside glass another polish with a dry cloth and then proceed to fill the tank three-quarters full with freshly-drawn water warmed to around 80°F. This is the final filling and the one we must take the greatest care with; be careful that you don't disturb the tank. Allow the water to run before filling the aquarium. This is to eliminate the possibility of water picking up metals from the pipes.

One method enabling you to fill the tank quickly with a minimum of disturbance is to stand a large pickle or cookie jar on top of a saucer or plate in the aquarium; fill the jar with water and as you continue to pour, the stream will run gently over the sides down the outside of the jar via the saucer into the tank, the main force being taken by the jar. If you have a tap that allows you to mix both hot and cold water, then a simpler method and much faster way is to connect your garden hose to this and "trickle" the water via the hose onto the inside aquarium glass. Be sure the water is only lukewarm or you may run the risk of cracking the glass. Do not run in cold water and then heat up with hot — cold water chills the plants and sets them back.

The reason you do not fill the tank right to the brim at this stage is to allow replacement of the odd plant that may float to the surface during the filling operation or the setting into place of some final ornament. Underwater, both plants and rocks will take on quite a different aspect and any alterations should be completed now; do not wait until the aquarium is completely full. If you fill it to the brim, inserting your arm to make some alteration will displace water all over the floor. This is a small point, yet it is amazing how many forget and

Vallisneria *in a tank that was set up with care. Photo by R. Zukal.*

end up with a ruined carpet.

When everything is ship-shape you can position the floating plants on the water and fill the tank until the water line just disappears behind the top frame of the aquarium. It is disconcerting to see so many set-ups only partly filled with water. While those who follow this practice may put forth sound arguments as to why they do it, I like to see the tank full. It is a different matter if you are building a terrarium or vivarium; half filling with water then is not only logical but very necessary to the well-being of the inhabitants, but we are constructing an aquarium and

An interesting aquascaping scheme is the terraced effect—low in front and higher toward the rear.

need as much swimming space as possible for our fish.

Finishing Up

Place the reflector on top of the tank: if other lighting is being used and your tank is minus a cover, be sure to fit a cover glass. Keep the glass just above the rim of the tank either by using clips (purchased at your dealer) or else by running strips of plastic tubing or rubber weather stripping around the edge of the glass. If you have cut the sheet of glass yourself, smooth off the edges.

Before placing the glass or reflector in place, slide the thermometer down the inside front glass with the calibrations towards the front for easy reading. About halfway down is fine. Next, connect your heater, lights and air pump to the power supply. Start your filter siphon and adjust the flow of air through the aerator.

Now you can stand back and survey the results of your handiwork. Pour yourself a cup of coffee and relax; you deserve it.

You must refrain from introducing fish to the aquarium for at least two days. Use this period to check that everything is working correctly and that the water temperature is constant at about 75°F. Those who use incandescent bulbs for illumination will find that after long periods this type of lighting tends to heat the water. Don't mistake this for a malfunctioning thermostat.

A slight tendency towards cloudiness in the water is quite natural at first and is part of the balancing process. This cloudiness should disappear after a while. Let it alone and the aquarium will repay you by taking on a crystal clarity.

Feeding

As feeders, fishes can be separated into three groups: the *carnivorous,* who prefer the meaty, live foods; the *herbivorous,* who prefer a menu laced with vegetable matter; and the *omnivorous,* who will eat almost anything! This doesn't mean that the carnivorous fish won't touch vegetation, or that the herbivores won't attack the daphnia. In fact, very hungry fish will soon modify their eating habits.

The tales about the so-called "fussy feeders" seem to stem

Live Food

A nourishing diet is just as important as keeping the environment right. The best diets are those that come as near as possible to what the aquatic animals feed on in their natural environment, but as we have already read, animals kept in captivity will quickly modify their feeding habits. Though smaller fishes do form a major part in the diet of fishes in the wild, they also eat small creatures, some of which can be purchased at your aquatic store or collected by the

A young Butterfly Fish, Pantodon buchholzi. *This species is adapted to a surface existence, and shows a strong preference for floating insects as food; sinking items will seldom be pursued. Photo by H. J. Richter.*

from a lack of understanding regarding how the fish like to feed. A bottom feeding catfish would have to be very hungry indeed to take his food in the open water in the middle of the tank, and a surface feeder such as the Butterfly Fish *(Pantodon buchholzi),* who likes his food served up on the water surface, would rarely venture down to the bottom in search of something to quell its appetite. Study the shapes of their mouths and you will get some idea of how they feed best.

aquarist. These we now discuss as live foods.

In feeding live natural foods we must consider the relationship between the size of the food animal and the fish to which it is offered. It is no use giving the small ciliates to the large cichlids although they are ideal for newly born fry. Feeding a community of small tropicals with whole earthworms would be equally useless. The fish in both cases would starve despite the apparent "abundance" of food in the tank.

Newly born fishes can take

Brine Shrimp (*Artemia salina*)

A young Crenicichla lepidota. *Pike cichlids are voracious predators and frequently refuse to accept anything but live fishes as food. Photo by U. Werner.*

ciliates (infusorians), newly hatched brine shrimp, and microworms.

Those live foods suitable for adult fish are adult brine shrimp, cyclops, daphnia, fly larvae, fruitflies, and worms such as grindal, white, or tubifex. Earthworms are excellent, but they must be chopped for all but the very large fish.

Brine shrimp, daphnia, cyclops, bloodworms, glass larvae and tubifex will last for several days to several weeks if kept in the refrigerator. The water should be changed daily and the container left uncovered, or at least perforated, for ventilation. Brine shrimp must be kept in salt water.

Brine Shrimp (*Artemia salina*)

These may be purchased as eggs which the hobbyist has to hatch out himself. The two major areas that provide these eggs are the salt flats around the Great Salt Lake in Utah, and the San Francisco Bay area in California. A third major source is western Canada. Eggs from Utah are usually darker in appearance. There are two methods for hatching out the shrimp — the shallow pan and the hatcher, the latter depending on a vigorous air stream to keep the eggs agitated.

Obtain an old pickle jar or other large jar that has been thoroughly cleaned with baking soda and water. To one gallon of water, add 6 tablespoons of non-iodized salt — cooking salt, sea, bay or kosher salt will do — and one tablespoon of Epsom salts (magnesium sulfate) and a pinch of bicarbonate of soda.

Place an air stone inside the jar

muslin and rinse in the tank where they are being fed.

To grow them to adult size you must prepare a separate container full of the brine solution. Bubble air through this slowly. Feed the growing shrimp with either green water or cream a small portion of yeast into the brine. Don't overdo this feeding or you will foul the brine and kill the shrimp.

Artemia are disease and parasite free, and make a wonderful food at any size, although the nauplii are more nutritious than the adults. Constant feeding with shrimp will slowly increase the salinity of the aquarium water, but if the partial change of water is carried out no harmful effects should be experienced. Many stores stock live and frozen adult brine shrimp.

on a long stem and connect it to a pump giving a good flow of air. When the brine solution is bubbling fiercely, sprinkle brine shrimp eggs on the surface (enough to cover a half dollar).

Place the hatcher in a warm spot about 75°F. In about 24 hours the shrimp will have hatched out. The speed of the growth depends on the temperature of the mixture as well as the area from which the eggs were collected and their subsequent processing. A temperature lower than 75°F would necessitate a longer period of growth. At a higher temperature this period is shorter.

To harvest, simply stop the aerator and place a low wattage light bulb over the hatcher. The egg cases will fall to the bottom and the newly hatched shrimp, attracted by the light, will swim to the surface. Siphon them out through a fine net or piece of

Hypostomus sp., showing the fleshy lips and rasping teeth that make these catfishes excellent algae cleaners in the aquarium. Photo by U. Werner.

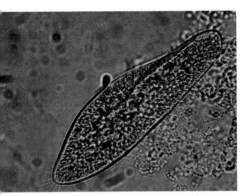

Paramecium *are among the protozoa and included in the catch-all term "infusoria." These are excellent food for very tiny fry. Photo by C. O. Masters.*

Ciliates
Paramecium caudatum:
Commonly called, because of its shape, the slipper animalcule, this is just one of a large group of semi-microscopic sized, one-celled protozoans that propel themselves through the water by means of tiny hairs called cilia. They can be collected from their natural habitats or bred in cultures at home. Because of their size, they are suitable for feeding the fry of only certain species. For years, aquarists have made infusoria cultures from a variety of things like hay, lettuce leaves and the like. These cultures were inoculated with ciliates and, hopefully, they bred. Lacking the necessary equipment for microscopic examination of his cultures, the fishkeeper often added them willy-nilly to his tanks and, in the process, added more bacteria than infusoria! Because of this danger, I much prefer to offer fry Euglena as their first food.

Euglena viridis: This is a tiny flagellate about 0.1 mm or less in length, found in profusion in freshwater ponds. In quantity, they form a greenish scum on the water surface. Euglena contain chlorophyll, the green pigment found in plants and, like the latter, give off oxygen and take in carbon dioxide, a point in their favor because they can live in the aquarium in large numbers without depreciating its oxygen content. To produce them in numbers one doesn't need intricate and costly laboratory equipment; in fact, most of what you need can be found around the house.

Boil half a pint of water in a small pan. When the water is bubbling vigorously, add a handful of wheat. Boil this for another ten minutes, then pour off the liquid. Place the wheat grains in a clean sterilized bottle with a narrow neck and add a cupful of cold water. Cork the bottle with a plug of absorbent cotton. Place this in a dark spot at room temperature for about two weeks, shaking the bottle daily to break up the surface scum that forms. At the same time remove the cotton plug for a few seconds, then replace it. If the plug gets wet, use a fresh, dry piece.

Collect your culture by skimming the green scum from a pond. If this isn't possible, certain biological supply houses will sell you an inoculation of Euglena. Add this to the liquid in the bottle. Now place it in a bright light and in a few days the contents will turn a bright green. Feed this liquid to your baby fishes. Replace the quantity removed with fresh water and put the culture back in the light. This will insure a ready source of Euglena

The common goldfish is a standard food for many large cichlids and other fishes with predatory leanings. Photo by Andre Roth.

baby food with no foul odors and very little fuss.

Cyclops

Named after a mythological one-eyed giant, this small crustacean is often found in daphnia cultures, where it is easily distinguished from the daphnia with a magnifying glass. A little experience will enable you to differentiate its swift, jerky movements from the sedate locomotion of the daphnia. It is frowned upon by some aquarists who claim it attaches itself to fishes. I have fed mine cyclops for over twenty years, and I have yet to observe this phenomenon. The fishes seem to find the two tiny egg sacs that the cyclops tows, a rare delicacy. If daphnia and cyclops are kept together, the former tends to disappear and one is left with a culture of cyclops only. Caught in ponds by using a fine net, they reach a length of 5 mm, which is suitable for the community aquarium.

Insect Larvae

Many species of fly larvae make good fish foods because they are found in abundance and are easy to net. The commonest used by the aquarist are the glass or phantom larvae (Corethra plumicornis), bloodworms (Chironomus plumosus), mosquito and gnat larvae, and Drosophila or fruitflies.

Phantom Larvae: Also called glassworms because they are so transparent. They float

A group of cyclopid copepods, usually known to hobbyists as Cyclops.

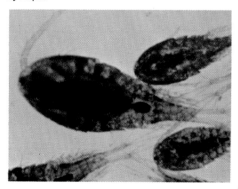

Daphnia are tiny crustaceans that can often be collected in ponds or drainage ditches with a fine dipnet.

their bright red coloration. Often found in daphnia cultures, they are found abundantly in polluted waters — usually being prolific in water receiving the waste from factories. Many people find them to be an excellent and nutritious dietary supplement for their fishes.

Fruitflies: *(Drosophila melanogaster):* The tiny flies are eagerly taken by most fish, particularly the surface feeders. Breed the wingless varieties, though the broods aren't quite as large as those of the winged fruit fly. They are easy to keep in jars. Feed them on over-ripe fruit, such as ripe bananas. To feed the fish, simply shake some of the flies onto the surface of the tank.

horizontally in the water and propel themselves by sharp twisting movements. Adults reach up to ½ inch in length and favor the surface areas of clear pools. Do not feed these if fry or eggs are present in the tank.

Bloodworms: Larvae of a chironomid midge they are not — technically — a worm at all. "Blood" fits them because of

Worms

The smallest of this family suitable for food are the **microworms** *(Anguillula silusae).* Excellent for young fishes, the fry of the livebearers will take them at birth. These worms, whitish in color, are cultured in a medium consisting of nine parts baby oatmeal, one part yeast, and

Mealworms are easy to raise in quantity and are good for surface-feeding fishes such as Pantodon buchholzi. *Photo by Michael Gilroy.*

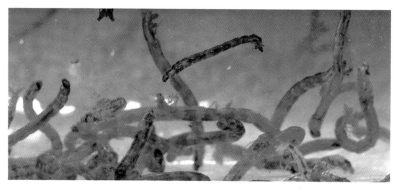

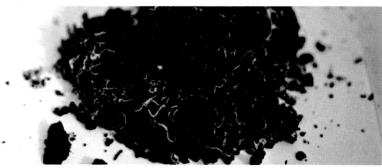

Top: "Bloodworms" are not worms at all, but rather the larvae of chironomid midges. Photo by Michael Gilroy. *Bottom:* Whiteworms or enchytraeids are easily cultured in soil. Photo by C. O. Masters.

enough water to make a loose paste. To this mixture add a starter culture purchased from your aquatic dealer. Kept in the dark in shallow dishes at a temperature around 73°F, microworms are prolific and crawl out of the culture and up the sides of the dish. Two blocks of wood with two nails driven into them to act as feet are placed in the mixture. Across the top of the two blocks is placed a sheet of glass and the dish is covered with another piece of glass. The microworms have an affinity for wet wood and will crawl up each block and cover the underside of the first glass. Feeding is achieved by rinsing this piece of glass in the aquarium. As cultures only have a limited life before they go sour, mix up a fresh oatmeal culture after a few days, and inoculate it with a spoonful of worms from the old set-up. Keep the culture in the dark when not in use.

Grindal worms *(Enchytraeus buchholzi):* Introduced from Sweden in 1949 by Frau Mortimer Grindal, hence their name. These small whiteworms fill the gap in size between the micro and the larger whiteworm. Fill a shallow wooden box with a mixture of peat and soil, moistened slightly. Place the culture of worms in a depression in the middle of the soil and cover it with either bread soaked in water (do not use milk for this purpose, as it quickly sours), oatmeal or moistened breakfast cereal. Press this down with a sheet of glass large enough to fit inside the box and cover this with a sheet of newsprint to keep out the light. Store in a dark place at room temperature. Allow the culture to stand for a few days. When the glass is lifted the worms will be seen congregating in clumps under the glass. Pick them off, rinse away the soil and feed to the fish. See that it is kept moist and that plenty of food is available, and the culture will last indefinitely. If the soil becomes infested with flies or larvae, eradicate them as follows:

feed too many white worms to your fish, as the worms are very rich in fat and if fed too frequently the fish will become obese. Keep the culture a little cooler than for Grindal. A starter culture of worms can be bought, but a search around the base of trees, especially under rotting pieces of bark, will usually reveal enough to start with.

Earthworms (*Lumbricus terrestris*): Though not strictly fed as "live" food, these worms are so easy to obtain and so nutritious that they should figure,

Meal moth larvae. Photo by C. O. Masters.

Remove the paper and glass and place the box in a bright light; after a short time the Grindal worms will have moved to the bottom of the box away from the source of light. When the top soil is clear of worms pass a flaming paper or blowtorch over it. This will quickly kill any flies, etc.

Whiteworms (*Enchytraeus albidus*): Larger relative of Grindal, reaching up to one inch. Culture as for the above. Do not

where possible, in the complete diet. After a rain shower, you will find dozens of garden worms on the surface of the earth. These can be cultured under burlap sacks in the garden. Feed them kitchen scraps. The usual way to present these worms to one's fish is by chopping them up. This is not a method relished by most fishkeepers. Try this: first rinse the worms under the tap. Then place a handful of worms in a

Tubifex worms, live or freeze-dried, are an excellent food for fishes and are usually accepted with gusto by all but the most finicky of fishes. Photo by C. O. Masters.

plastic bag and place this in the refrigerator for about fifteen minutes, just enough time to chill them but not long enough for them to freeze solid. Then, keeping the worms in the bag on a hard, flat surface, crush them into a thin layer. Return them to the refrigerator and freeze this solid. When needed, all you have to do is peel some of the plastic bag and break off a small portion, grating this into the aquarium.

A female cyclopid copepod. Note the egg sacs attached to the posterior portion of the body.

Like Daphnia, earthworms tend to be laxative, so feed sparingly.

Tubifex There are several genera and species. They are all thin red worms, up to one inch long, found in great numbers carpeting the beds of ditches and slow-moving rivers. Burying the head portion in the mud, they wave their posterior parts about in search of food. They are obtainable from most pet shops and are sold in live portions that resemble pieces of wriggling red meat. Tubifex quickly congregate into a ball and won't keep very long unless kept under running water. The best way is to place them on a shallow dish or saucer and keep under a dripping tap. Otherwise, the water covering the worms must be changed frequently or the worms will die. Do not feed any worms that have lost their color or are very thin and long. Feed to the aquarium inhabitants by dropping a few worms at a time into the tank, or use a worm feeder.

They are suitable for most aquarium fishes, but don't overdo the feeding. Surplus worms drop to the bed of the aquarium and form a mass, or even burrow into the gravel where it is difficult for all but the bottom feeders to reach them. They can be collected from the wild, but the process of separating them from the mud is messy and not worth the trouble. They are usually available all year round from your dealer. For the very tiny fish, chop the tubifex by placing a lump of them into an *enamel* bowl with no water, and cut repeatedly into the ball of the worms with the tips of a sharp pair of scissors. Another method is to place a portion on a wooden board and slice it with a razor blade.

Frozen and Freeze-Dried Foods

Many foods such as brine shrimp, daphnia, and tubifex can be purchased as a frozen block. Treat these the same way as human frozen foods. Don't allow the complete pack to thaw out; break off a sufficient amount for each feed and quickly replace the balance into the freezer. If you

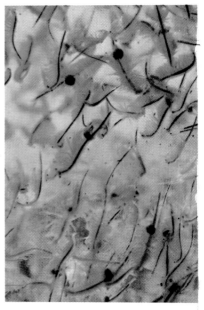

One of the most versatile of all fish foods is brine shrimp, Artemia salina. Available live, frozen, or freeze-dried, it is an excellent staple in the diet of aquarium fishes. Photo by C. O. Masters.

Frozen foods offer a wide range of choices to the aquarist, including some foods that contain a relatively high quantity of vegetative materials to make them appeal to essentially vegetarian species as well as meat-eaters. Photo courtesy of Ocean Nutrition.

Pelleted aquarium foods are available in pellet sizes to cover both small and large (and in-between-size) species and in both sinking and floating forms. Photo courtesy of Hikari.

wrap the pack in several layers of newspapers when bringing them home from the shop, they will not thaw out on the way.

Freeze-dried foods, which look like small pieces of leather, are an important innovation in fish feeding. Such foods as shrimp, tubifex, and liver are all available in frozen dried form. Feeding is simply a matter of sticking a small piece of the food to the inside glass of the tank where the fishes can pick at it. It is a good way to feed liver, but use only small portions at a time or you will cloud the water. Freeze-dried products have an advantage in that they don't need refrigeration.

Dry Food

Though everyone generally agrees that live foods such as daphnia, cyclops, tubifex, and so

Flake foods are a convenient and popular means of feeding aquarium fishes. They offer a very wide range of foods and a very large range of package sizes. Photo courtesy of Hagen.

on, are the best complete foods, dried packaged foods do have their use and act as roughage to aid the digestion. Manufacturers spend much time and money in research before their dried foods are put on the market, and today's hobbyist can take his pick from a profusion of packaged diets. In the cradle period of the tropical fish hobby, aquarists were perfectly satisfied to feed their pets on a monotonous menu of dried ant's eggs. In fact, some goldfish fanciers still do! These shriveled-up larvae and egg cases (usually to be had in the cheap range of packaged foods) add little to the intake of the fish but bulk.

Dried foods have certain disadvantages. Food left uneaten will fall to the bottom of the aquarium, where it lodges in cracks and crevices. When the fish do not eat it, it goes foul very quickly in the heated water of the tropical aquarium. Bacteria feed on this decay and can multiply to such an extent that they form clouds in the water. Result? The oxygen in the water is rapidly used up, and the fish are found

gasping atmospheric oxygen at the surface of the water. Even the use of aeration and filtration cannot relieve the situation when it has reached this stage.

Some foods lose an appreciable amount of their nutritional value during the cooking and drying processes to which most of these dried foods are subjected. Dried foods, particularly those cheap mixed foods produced by unreliable sources occasionally become infested with tiny bugs and their larvae. Though these, for the most part, won't harm the fish if fed to them, they aren't very pleasant to have around the home.

Dried foods come in a profusion of varieties and grades, the three basic grades being Coarse, Medium, and Fine. Most of the finely powdered foods are suitable for feeding only to the very young fish; the larger species can consume fine foods only by sucking, and many will refuse to bother if the particles are too small. Crab and shrimp meal come in powder or coarse grade, but beware of the large package of powdered or ground shrimp offered at a suspiciously cheap price. To sell at this figure the manufacturer usually has to grind up the complete shrimp, not just the meat. Consequently it contains fine shell which is less nutritious than the meat.

Flake foods are best purchased large, then rubbed down with the fingers to a size suitable for the fish. They are best when they remain floating on the water surface for long periods. Unless bottom feeders are present, be wary of food that sinks rapidly.

The secrets of feeding dried

eating catfishes who must have vegetables as an integral part of their diet. Lettuce leaves chopped into the tank have been suggested, but the author does not favor lettuce too often because the decaying leaves produce large numbers of ciliates. Spinach is better. Peas, when cooked, are excellent if the hard outer shell is first removed. Crush a quantity of cooked peas in the hand, squeezing out as much moisture as possible, then bottle the crushed peas and use when required. Sometimes floating

Like dry foods, frozen foods such as these Lifeline products from Biotope Research, Inc. also are available in many different forms.

food are moderation and variety. Though not complete foods, they suffice where time is important to the hobbyist and the availability of live foods, either purchased or collected, is in doubt.

Vegetable Diets

Though most species will browse on the plants and green algae growths in the tank, there are some like those of *Metynnis*, some cyprinids, and the algae-

plants like duckweed will be eaten.

Frequent Feedings

The average person eats three meals per day, and if he is in good health most meals result in clean plates. Imagine that one day you skip the first two meals. Arriving home in the evening, your wife sets the contents of all three meals in front of you. I doubt very much that even an appetite

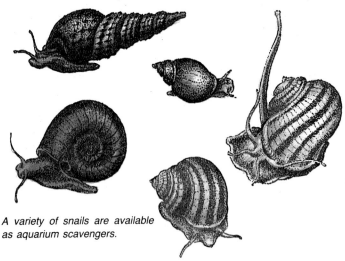

A variety of snails are available as aquarium scavengers.

sharpened by a day's abstinence could face all that food at one sitting! Yet this is just what many fishkeepers expect their fish to do. Usually when the fish can be fed only in the evening, a large helping of food is tipped into the aquarium (all three meals at once). After a time our hobbyist wonders why his tank is never clean. Healthy fish consume food in small portions all day long, but they can eat only so much at a time. Feeding large portions is bound to cause problems.

Feed as often as is possible, but only what can be consumed by the occupants in a few minutes. If circumstances permit personal feeding only in the evening, either recruit the aid of the family to feed them when you are absent, or feed live foods that will live on in the tank for a long period of time.

Variety

I love strawberries and cream! No doubt you too have your favorite food. Yet if I were to eat strawberries and cream for breakfast, lunch, and dinner, I would very quickly hate the sight of them. For fish too, variety is the

spice of life, and this does not mean just a change in brand names. Too many fishkeepers buy one brand of food, feed it meal after meal until it is gone, and then switch to another brand, thinking they are feeding a varied diet. Most emphatically, they are not! Variety means varying the diet daily, feeding *all* the different types of food mentioned in this chapter.

When you return home with foods that are packed in perishable containers, either empty them into screw-top glass jars or buy yourself some little plastic boxes with tight fitting lids. Mark the date of purchase on the outside. This date will help you to keep an eye on the age of the food in the boxes. Don't indiscriminately mix different foods together; some foods can affect others. Liver spoils very quickly and can send "off" any other food it is mixed with. Throw away any foods that emit a musty odor, have developed fungus growths or have become riddled with insects or larvae. The smell of these foods attracts insects, so keep the lid tight at all times when not in use.

The Family Game — Breeding

As opposed to merely keeping fishes in an aquarium, breeding them is an enterprise requiring planning, preparation and attention to certain conditions. The hobbyist must learn about the requirements and conditions conducive to the mating of his particular fishes. Knowing this, he influence of internal secretions and external environmental conditions, spawning is just a part of the natural life cycle of the fish. The breeding cycles of temperate zone creatures are influenced by seasonal lengthening and shortening of the daylight hours. Fortunately for us, the majority of

Breeding fishes is always a rewarding endeavor. Most species display their best color when spawning. Witness the striking color of this male Dwarf Gourami, Colisa lalia, *one of the most beautiful aquarium fishes. Photo by H. J. Richter.*

can create in his aquarium an environment which simulates — as nearly as possible — the necessary "natural" conditions that encourage fish to breed. Other than that, there are no "secrets" to fish breeding. Simply pay attention to the last detail, making sure, of course, that the chosen pair are male and female — ready to spawn.

Stimulated or triggered by the fishes kept in an aquarium are not seasonal, and they will breed throughout the year if conditions are right.

Basic Principles
Concerning water conditions in the breeding tank, they should be similar to those found by the fish in their home waters. If they came from soft, acid waters, it is no use

expecting them to breed in tanks containing hard, alkaline water. The salts causing the hard, alkaline conditions would merely destroy the outer casing of the eggs and render them infertile. Probably one of the main reasons why we still tag fish "difficult to breed" is that we lack knowledge regarding their natural environment.

It goes without saying that the fish in question must be a pair. Though this may seem an obvious condition to the beginner, further aquatic experience will prove just how hard some species of fish are to sex successfully. Always try to breed fish that have paired off naturally in the aquarium and are displaying the behavior associated with the mating act.

Reference has been made to a separate "breeding tank." This doesn't imply that fish won't or can't be bred in the community aquarium. In the case of some livebearers it would be difficult to stop them, but a separate tank enables the aquarist to carefully control the environment and also to adopt methods of saving the eggs from the cannibalistic tendencies of the tank inhabitants. Just as we humans

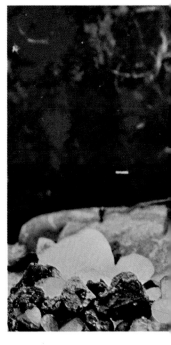

Killifishes such as Nothobranchius korthausae *(top) typically lay eggs on plants or bury them in the substrate, cichlids like* Pelvicachromis pulcher *(bottom), however, carefully tend the eggs and fry. Upper photo by H. J. Richter, lower by B. Kahl.*

class "caviar" as a desirable food, so do fishes. Nothing is more disheartening to the would-be breeder than to see the results of his carefully laid plan — the prestigious eggs or fry — being consumed by adult fish.

Take suitable precautions after the production of fry or eggs to see that the resultant young fish are raised properly. Feeding is critical in their first few days of life, and the breeder has to provide sufficient food for their wants but not so much that it fouls the water.

Methods of Reproduction

[a] Viviparous — giving birth to *live* young that have developed from eggs within the body of the mother and have been nourished from her bloodstream.

[b] Oviparous — producing eggs which hatch *outside* the mother's body, expelled by her and fertilized by milt from the male during spawning.

[c] Ovoviviparous — producing eggs that hatch within the mother's body. They are unlike viviparous species in that the eggs do not receive nourishment from the mother's bloodstream.

Therefore, we can divide our fishes into two major categories: *livebearers* and *egglayers.* The latter, which form the larger group, are further subdivided according to the methods employed in spawning:

[i] *Egg Scatterers:* The female drops her eggs all over the tank, willy-nilly, and the male fertilizes them with a covering of male sperm or milt.

[ii] *Egg Adherers:* Fishes which drop adhesive or semi-sticky eggs that are "anchored" to various sites; the parents have no further interest in them once they are ejected and fertilized.

[iii] *Egg Tenders:* Similar to [ii] but after (carefully) depositing the eggs on a pre-determined site the parents (carefully) look after them.

[iv] *Mouthbrooders:* After spawning takes place the eggs are picked up in the mouth by one of the parents (which parent depends on the species). Here they incubate and are expelled as free-swimming fry.

*Guppies are livebearers. **Left:** fancy Guppies. Photo by H. Kyselov. **Top:** Female Guppy giving birth. Photo by H. J. Richter.*

[v] *Bubblenest Builders:* An elaborate surface nest of bubbles sometimes including bits of plant and tank debris is constructed. The eggs are deposited in the nest, after which they are looked after either by the male alone or by both parents until the eggs hatch.

[vi] *Substratum or Egg Buriers:* Probably the most unusual and interesting method of all is the one in which the eggs are buried in mud.

The Fishes

Like human beings, fishes have backbones and are therefore classified as belonging to the "chordates." In point of fact, with more than 40,000 separate species on record, they form the largest group of the animals with backbones or endoskeletons. Of these, we primarily maintain in our aquaria those coming under the heading of the Teleosts.

Where these spiny and soft rays occur together in one fin (Percidae, etc.), the fin count can be expressed thus: D.VI, 12-13, meaning that the dorsal fin in this particular fish contains six spiny rays and twelve to thirteen soft rays.

Skin

Fish skin consists of two layers, a

Fins

Fin function provides some of the power to propel the fish through the water, contributing to steering and stability. As the number and shape of these fins help in identification, it is well to learn their names.

The majority of fishes have seven fins; three single fins called *dorsal* (top), *caudal* (tail), and *anal* (under); and two paired sets referred to as ventral (under) and *pectorals* (breast). In some fishes the top dorsal fin is divided into two; the rays at the front of this fin are known as hard or spiny, and their numbers are expressed by *Roman* numerals; the remainder of the rays are soft and designated by *Arabic* figures.

Top: Cichlids such as this Fire-mouth have well-developed fins for excellent maneuverability. Photo by A. van den Nieuwenhuizen. *Left:* This Knifefish moves by waving a modified anal fin, but due to the reduction or absence of other fins, it is not very maneuverable. *Bottom:* Gars such as Lepisosteus oculatus *can move very quickly due to powerful fins and a torpedo-shaped body. Photo by Dr. Herbert R. Axelrod.*

thin outer layer (epidermis), made up of simple cells which are constantly being worn away and renewed, and a thicker inner layer (dermis) consisting of a complicated mingling of muscle fibers and blood vessels. Mucous glands permeate both layers to produce a protective coating over the body of the fish. This "slime" not only helps to streamline the fish, it protects it from attack by bacteria, parasites and fungi. Never use dry hands or dry nets when handling fish, or you may damage this layer, leaving the fish open to infection.

Scales
The scales overlap each other like the shingles on a house and consist of four kinds: cycloid, ctenoid, ganoid, and placoid. Scale counts are used to identify the different species of fish, particularly in closely related genera. There are two ways to count scales. The first is along the lateral line. The second is the transverse count — count the numbers of scales running obliquely from the dorsal to the

anal fin.

In appearance, scales are not dissimilar to the cross section taken through a tree trunk for, like the latter, they possess "rings" which give a guide to age. As each fish scale develops, it forms a circle. During the winter when growth slows down, irregular circles, called annuli, are formed. Counting these will give the approximate age.

Muscular System

If you remove the scales and outer skin from a fish and expose the flesh beneath, you will observe zig-zag lines running transversely around the body. These are the *myotomes,* divided by the tissue *myosepta.* Imagine a series of paper cups fitting one within the other. These provide the muscle action used in propulsion. The gill arches, jaws and operculum are actuated by other, weaker muscles.

Eyes

The spherical lenses in the eyes of fishes enable them to see in the semi-darkness of the water. Having monocular vision, fishes can see in two directions, but are incapable of focusing both eyes on the same object at the same time. When stationary, objects up to a foot and a half away can be brought into accurate focus, but fishes are aware of objects much farther away from them than this. One of the oddities concerning unusual vision in fishes are the *Anableps* species. These creatures live at the surface of water. Their eyes are divided into two parts, enabling them to see both above and below the water at the same time and on two sides, as well.

Gills

These may be called the "lungs" of the fish. Water is taken in through the mouth and passed over the gill filaments, where an exchange of gases takes place: the oxygen is extracted and the spent gases of respiration (primarily carbon dioxide) are expired. In the labyrinth fishes *(Anabantidae),* as well as in a few other genera, there is an extra

Right: A "Serpae" Tetra, Hyphessobrycon *sp. Photo by H. J. Richter.* **Bottom:** An armored catfish, Hoplosternum thoracatum. *Photo by R. Zukal.*

Killifishes are visual predators and thus have well-developed eyes. Photo of Aplocheilus lineatus *by H. J. Richter.*

respiratory organ enabling them to breathe at the water surface and, in the case of the climbing perch, even to live out of the water! The gills are protected by a movable outer cover called the *operculum.*

Mouth
The mouth is usually large and comes in many forms, each reflecting the eating habits of that particular species. Teeth too are intimately connected with diet, varying in location, shape and function. Some teeth are positioned on the jaws, tongue, or the palatine bones of the mouth; the actual mastication of the food is performed by the pharyngeal teeth in the throat.
Some species have mouths modified into a sucker, enabling them to cling to rocks or the glass sides of the aquarium. Many of the *Hypostomus* catfishes from South America have this ability.

Nostrils
Fish perceive odors through sensory tissues in the nares (nostrils). The stimulation so received is passed via the nerves to the *olfactory* portion of the brain. Smell plays a very important part in the identification of food, particularly in the case of the Blind Cave Fish *(Astyanax fasciatus mexicanus)* deprived of the sense of sight.

Lateral Line
The lateral line is visible as a series of dots along each side of a fish. This actually consists of a series of sense organs called *neuromasts* which extend from behind the head to the base of the caudal fin. Via a sunken canal, they are connected through pores in the scales. The lateral line is sensitive to low pressure waves and supplements the sensory

systems of the olfactory and visual senses.

Swim Bladder

This is similar in function to the ballast tanks aboard a submarine that are filled with water to submerge the boat. In the air bladder of the fish a combination of oxygen, nitrogen and carbon dioxide is used to inflate or deflate. This organ adjusts the weight of the fish in relation to the amount of water its body is displacing, allowing it to rise or sink. Sometimes intestinal troubles give rise to malfunction of this organ, and as a result, the fish cannot control its movements. It loses its balance and usually lies on its side, swimming up only with an effort. Some fishes, such as the North American darters, lack this useful organ and so usually spend their time on the bottom.

Do Fishes Feel Pain?

Whether they do or not is a very debatable and controversial point among everyone from angler to ichthyologist. We have read that fish have an elaborate system of nerves and sensory organs and the presence of these suggests that they feel something. Experiments have proved that some species are more sensitive than others, but not whether these feelings include pain. Only another fish could speak authoritatively on this subject! However, it has been observed that when fish experience internal stimulation such as when they are feeding or spawning, their sensitivity to external stimuli is reduced.

Do Fishes Sleep?

The absence of eyelids, so that their eyes cannot be closed, leads many people to conclude that fish in the aquarium do not sleep. Observations, however, have proved that fish go into a state of suspended animation akin to sleep. When the tank is plunged into darkness, many of the fish will lie motionless on the gravel or plant leaves and in some cases even flat horizontally in the water, remaining in this trance-like state for long periods. The exceptions to this are the nocturnal animals.

Why Cold-blooded?

Fishes have a body temperature

controlled by the temperature of their environment. If the temperature of the water in the aquarium is increased, then the metabolism of the fish is quickened and they eat more and become more active. Find the right temperature range to suit the species you keep, as increasing the temperature too much will shorten the life span of the fish. A drop in temperature slows down the body functions, making the fish listless, without appetite, and subject to disease. Unless the condition is corrected the fish will die; 75°F is considered a good median temperature.

Nomenclature

"It's all Greek to me!" is the usual outcry when the fishkeeper comes up against the Latin or Greek scientific names of the fishes. Why bother with the difficult-to-pronounce, hard-to-spell scientific names? Why not use the common name of "guppy," rather than the hard-to-remember *Poecilia reticulata* (*Poecilia* = many colored; *reticulata* = netlike)? The answer lies in the fact that scientific names serve several useful purposes and simplify identification of species — and,

like it or not, they are here to stay!

In the U.S., for example, several ground squirrels, at least twenty other rodents, a snake, and a tortoise share the common name of Gopher. However, each of these creatures has a separate and distinct scientific name, enabling us to distinguish one from the other. These names also explain the relationship of various creatures, one to another.

Just as most civilized humans have two names, so do fishes. Let us look once more at the Guppy, *Poecilia reticulata*. *Poecilia* is the generic name. Only the generic name begins with a capital letter. It can be applied to many related fish just as we have many Smiths and Joneses; *reticulata* refers to the specific species.

Guppies are live-bearing fishes just like Mollies, Platies and Swordtails, to mention but a few, and all these come under the family name Poeciliidae. Finally, one may come across yet another name following these two; this is the name of the person who first described and classified this particular species, for example, *Poecilia reticulata* Peters.

The confused beginner can take heart in the fact that the scientists themselves often find it just as difficult.

Rasbora maculata. *Photo by B. Kahl.*

Fish Catalog

Between 1500 and 2000 species, subspecies, and varieties of fishes have passed through, or are being kept in tropical fish hobbyist aquariums throughout the world. Obviously, it is beyond the scope of a beginner's book to list and fully describe all of these species. Many of them are rare, others are difficult to keep, while still others lack color, have bad habits, or for other reasons are not popular.

In this catalog of fishes the author intends to list and briefly limited to those features and requirements most likely to be of use to the hobbyist in maintaining and breeding the species. The sizes given are the maximum known for the species. Many will breed at considerably smaller sizes, and in many cases, the sizes given are applicable to fishes grown in a natural state; fishes grown in aquariums often mature at a considerably smaller size. The sex distinctions given are not necessarily the only ones, but those most likely to be

The most popular of the anabantoids is undoubtedly the Siamese Fighting Fish or Betta, Betta splendens. *Never mix two males of this species! Photo by Michael Gilroy.*

describe those fishes which are most suitable for the home aquarium and most likely to be available to the hobbyist. For the convenience of the hobbyist the families are listed alphabetically although scientifically it is not usually done this way.

The descriptions are necessarily brief and incomplete. However, the author believes that they will be of value to the hobbyist since they emphasize those details which will be most useful in recognizing a fish and in differentiating it from similar species.

The discussion of care also is noticeable to the hobbyist.

In general, sexing is done by an experienced observer on the basis of the overall appearance of the fish. With time and practice, it becomes almost intuitive. The author knows many old-time aquarists who glance at a fish and say it is either a male or a female but, when pressed for a reason, they are honestly unable to specify.

Family ANABANTIDAE

Labyrinth Fishes
The anabantoids are found in Africa and southern Asia. They

are distinguished by a special structure in the head which serves as an accessory breathing organ, from which they derive their name of "labyrinth fishes." This special adaptation permits labyrinth fishes to exist in waters which are deficient in oxygen. The most common illustration of this is the row of "Betta jars" so frequently seen at tropical fish dealers. These jars may hold anywhere from three ounces to a quart of water, and within each one is an individual Siamese Fighting Fish, not at all perturbed by the lack of surface area or the closeness of its quarters.

Every few minutes they rise majestically to the surface, leisurely gulping a mouthful of air; as they slowly sink, the exhausted air may be seen emerging as a bubble from their gills.

The majority of anabantoids are so-called "bubblenest builders." Sometimes the male, sometimes both parents, build a raft of bubbles at the surface. Frequently, this is free-floating, but many species prefer to anchor it to the plants. The eggs are deposited within this nest and usually guarded by the male, although occasionally the female will participate. As a rule, the female had best be removed, particularly if the male shows any signs of belligerence. Commercial breeders remove both parents in order to insure maximum hatching and rearing. However, for the aquarist one of the delights of tropical fish breeding is watching the care and attention lavished on the young by the parent. After all, our aquarium is being kept primarily for pleasure, not for profit.

Most of the anabantoids,

Colisa fasciata is usually known as the Giant Gourami even though it rarely exceeds four inches in length. Photo by Hansen.

A pair of Honey Gouramis, Colisa chuna, *in a spawning embrace beneath their bubblenest. Photo by H. J. Richter.*

originating as they do in hot, humid climates, prefer temperatures above 75°F, perhaps closer to 80°F. Their aquarium should also be well-covered to establish a warm humid area above the water surface. With the exception of the Siamese Fighting Fish *(Betta splendens),* the majority of anabantoids we are likely to encounter are fair to good community fishes and may be kept together. However, when they begin to show signs of pairing off, the happy couple had best be removed to a separate aquarium for breeding. The size of the aquarium, of course, is determined by the species. For example, *Colisa lalia,* the Dwarf Gourami, will feel perfectly at home in a five-gallon aquarium, while *Trichogaster trichopterus,* the Blue Gourami, will require at least a fifteen- to twenty-gallon aquarium. Some of the signs of spawning are increased color, a tendency to frequent one corner of the aquarium from which other fishes are being driven, and, of course, the building of the bubblenest. Once the bubblenest is built, the normal procedure is for the male, using a combination of enticement and drive, to bring the female underneath the nest where the eggs are laid and fertilized during the embrace. Certain anabantoids, such as the Dwarf Gourami, lay eggs which are lighter than water and will float up into the nest. It is interesting to note that those species which lay these light eggs will always maneuver so that they are directly under the nest during the embrace. The eggs of other species, such as the Betta, are heavier and will sink to the bottom.

The female floats torpidly after

the embrace, the eggs being gathered up by the male and spat into the nest. The embrace may be repeated a number of times over a period of hours. Egg-laying completed, the parent which is to do the guarding takes up its position under the nest and drives off all intruders. At a temperature of 80°F, hatching usually occurs within approximately thirty hours. The young hang vertically under the nest, absorbing their egg yolk. In another 24 to 48 hours they become free-swimming, at which time they require the finest of fine foods such as rotifers, algae, and other single-celled organisms. There are several commercial dried foods on the market prepared specifically for this type of fry. In another two or three days, the young should have grown enough to have graduated to newly-hatched brine shrimp, microworms, strained daphnia, etc.

Care should be taken not to disturb the parents during the breeding period, as otherwise they may forget their parental duties to the extent of eating the eggs or young. Temperature is also important during this period, as the fry are particularly sensitive to chills. Surprisingly enough, the fry are not born with the labyrinth. Its formation takes place several weeks after hatching, and until the time it is fully developed and activated the fry are dependent upon water absorbed through the gills, just as are the fry of other fishes.

Betta splendens — Siamese Fighting Fish

Originally imported from Malaya and Thailand, the Siamese Fighting Fish has a body length not much over 2 to 2½ inches. The full magnificence of the Siamese Fighting Fish or, as it is more usually called, the Betta, is in the intense coloration and magnificent finnage which adorn a show specimen like the sails of a full-rigged ship. The original Betta was a dark purplish-red fish, although occasionally a few color variations, notably the Cambodia (red fins on a white body), have been found. Today, almost all the hues of the rainbow are being bred ranging from a cellophane Betta, which is white with clear fins, through reds, blues, greens, lavenders, purples, and up to an almost black Betta. The female, however, unfortunately does not carry either the extreme coloration of the male nor his finnage. She resembles, even in spite of all the efforts of breeders, the original wild Betta, although she has increased slightly in size.

The name "Fighting Fish" is somewhat of a misnomer. While it is true that this fish will fight other males of his own species like a gamecock, he is relatively peaceful and slow-moving when kept in a community aquarium and rarely bothers other fishes. In fact, his gorgeous draperies often furnish a target for some of the nippier fishes. Nor will two male fighting fish, as a rule, fight to the death. Usually, the fight ends with the loser fleeing. Of course, in a small aquarium there is no place for him to hide and he may eventually be killed. In their native home of Thailand, they are used for sport, wagers being laid on the outcome of a fight. In Bangkok, the capitol of Thailand, almost every tourist stop has a hawker offering to show tourists

A striking red Betta with just a hint of blue iridescence. Photo by Michael Gilroy.

the Fighting Fish in combat for a fee. His fish are not really select specimens, but nondescript fishes picked up just for the purpose of entertaining the tourists. The show they put on usually leaves much ferocity to be desired.

Breeding takes place as given in the general description for the anabantoids, except that the male and female should not be put together except for breeding purposes. At other times, each male should be isolated or just one male kept in the community aquarium. The females, which are not belligerent, may be kept together or with other fishes.

Siamese Fighting Fish display their finest colors during breeding or when facing another male. Owners of these exotic fish put a small mirror in the aquarium when they want their fish to display their finery.

Colisa fasciata — Giant Gourami

Hailing from India and Thailand, this interesting and lovely gourami is misnamed — he is really not a giant. Seldom reaching a length of five inches, he will breed at only three inches. A deep-bodied fish, the ventral fins are elongated to form long thread-like feelers which serve as tactile organs. Unfortunately, this is one fish which does not show at its best until it has been established in an aquarium for some time.

Colisa labiosa — Thick-lipped Gourami

Coming from southern Burma, the Thick-lipped closely resembles the Giant Gourami in shape and coloration, but it is considerably smaller, attaining a length of only three inches. Like the Giant Gourami, it suffers from a

Top: The Pearl Gourami, Trichogaster leeri, *is one of the most attractive anabantoids. It reaches five inches but remains very peaceful.* **Left:** The Thick-lipped Gourami, Colisa labiosa, *is very similar to* C. fasciata. Photo by A. Roth.

misnomer. The lips are not actually noticeably thicker than that of other fishes of its type, although they do have a black ring which gives them an appearance of thickness. A somewhat retiring fish requiring high temperatures, under proper conditions the Thick-lipped becomes a deep

gorgeous blue-black, making it one of the most attractive fishes in the aquarium.

Colisa lalia — Dwarf Gourami
In the author's opinion, the Dwarf Gourami and the Honey Gourami must certainly vie for honors as the most beautiful of the anabantoids, and certainly among the most beautiful of the aquarium fishes. However, where the Honey reveals its coloring only under ideal conditions, the Dwarf Gourami consistently shows his alternately red and green vertical zig-zag stripes. This, together with a brilliant-blue breast and a gentle disposition, make him a must in almost any collection of mixed fishes. The female, unfortunately, does not display quite the brilliant coloring of the male although she is quite attractive in her own right. A deep-bodied fish, the Dwarf Gourami only reaches a length of 2 to 2½ inches.

Colisa chuna — Honey Gourami
The Honey is somewhat slimmer than the Dwarf Gourami, but approximately the same length — two to two and one-half inches. Beautiful, even when not displaying, the male is a dark brownish-red with a blue throat and chest, the color of which extends into the anal fin. Under ideal conditions, which include a high temperature and a well-planted aquarium, the red becomes a brilliant golden-red, and the blues glow with an electric quality which must be seen to be believed.

Helostoma temmincki — Kissing Gourami
Ranging extensively through southeast Asia, the Kissing Gourami reaches the rather large size (large, that is, for a popular aquarium fish) of up to ten inches. They are not very colorful, being a uniform light-pink or flesh-colored, with black eyes. The main reason that they are kept is the odd habit which gives them their name. Two kissers will pucker up and apparently osculate, sometimes holding that position for several minutes at a time. However, two males will

Kissing Gouramis, Helostoma temmincki, *doing what they do best. Actually, there is no affection involved here—it is likely that this is a form of ritual combat, and in fact the two fish involved are probably males.*

indulge in the practice as will two females. In fact, they are probably engaging in a kind of combat. It is interesting to watch, and the fish is fairly hardy if the water is kept at 75°F or above. Further, they do clean algae from the aquarium and are usually peaceful. For these reasons alone, they are well worth a place in our community tank.

Macropodus opercularis — Paradise Fish

Although several species of *Macropodus* have been kept in the aquarium from time to time, the red Paradise Fish and an albino version are the only ones which have achieved any degree of popularity. One of the earliest, if not the first, tropical fish kept in an aquarium, the Paradise Fish is hardy and interesting. It is one of the few anabantoids which doesn't mind a low temperature, frequently surviving as low as 40°F. They are ideal parents, breeding in typical anabantoid fashion, both caring for the fry. The author has frequently seen aquaria in which several broods of young have been raised, and it is interesting to watch both

Whereas some albinos are quite colorless, the albino strain of the Paradise Fish, Macropodus opercularis, *is quite attractive. Photo by Jaroslav Elias.*

Many color varieties of the Blue Gourami, Trichogaster trichopterus, *have been bred. This marbled form is known as the Opaline Gourami. Photo by H. J. Richter.*

parents caring for a nest containing eggs while the preceding, free-swimming batch swarms about.

Unfortunately, however, the male Paradise Fish only shows his beautiful blue and brick-red colors during breeding, being rather drab at other times. Also, he is inclined to be belligerent with smaller fishes although this belligerency has been exaggerated. All in all, however, it is a fish worth keeping by the beginner with adequate room. The fins of the male are extremely long and pointed, the anal and caudal in particular, extending into trailing filaments.

Trichogaster leeri — Pearl Gourami

One of the few larger fishes which may be safely kept with almost any size neighbor. Coming from southeast Asia, the Pearl Gourami reaches a length of almost five inches, but will breed at three. When in breeding colors, the male exhibits a deep orange breast. Basically, the body color is a light lavender with an overall opalescent or pearl gleam. A fine black zig-zag line extends from

The Moonlight Gourami, Trichogaster microlepis, *has small silvery scales that give the fish a pleasing shimmering effect. Photo by Gene Wolfsheimer.*

the mouth, through the eye, ending in a black spot at the base of the tail. The entire body and fins are covered with a series of dark reticulated markings. Both parents frequently participate in caring for the nest and young. The fins of the male are extremely elongated, particularly the anal and dorsal.

Trichogaster microlepis — Moonlight Gourami

This is a fairly attractive introduction from Thailand which reaches a length of almost six inches ;in spite of its large size and its rather quiet coloration, it is popular among specialists.

Trichogaster trichopterus — The Three-spot or Blue Gourami

A long-time favorite, this is another fairly large fish from southeast Asia, reaching a length of six inches. The coloring is a

Top: The Striped Headstander, Anostomus anostomus, is usually peaceful. Photo by A. Roth. Bottom: Leporinus fasciatus is a species that may be tough on live plants. Photo by H. Schultz.

rather dull, medium-dark gray-blue. The name was given because there is one spot in the center on the body, one at the base of the tail, and the eye forms the third. At one time quite popular, it has largely been replaced by aquarium strains such as the Blue Gourami, which is similar in size and shape but a much more colorful blue.

The Opaline or Cosby Gourami is merely a sport or mutant originating from the Blue Gourami. It resembles the Blue Gourami in size, form, and breeding behavior, the major difference being the dark blue, somewhat iridescent markings which overlay the basic blue body coloration.

Family ANOSTOMIDAE

**Abramites hypselonotus —
Marble Headstander**
A rather large (up to 5 inches) fish from the lower Amazon, with a distinctive nose-down swimming posture. Poorly defined, broad brown-gray and light ivory-yellow bands are found over the body. It is a fairly hardy fish, but is apt to be quarrelsome, particularly with others of its species.

***Anostomus anostomus* —
Striped Headstander**
This slim, five-inch fish has three

dark stripes running the length of the body which are interspersed with lighter lines. The fins are bright red in good specimens. Although not usually quarrelsome, it is a large fish best kept with others of equal size. Its

Chilodus punctatus

Abramites hypselopterus

habitat is near the headwaters of the Amazon.

***Chilodus punctatus* — Spotted Headstander**
Ranging throughout northern South America, this is a medium-sized (up to three-inch), attractive and peaceful, although unfortunately, somewhat delicate aquarium fish. The ground color is a pearl to light-purple. The scales are large, each scale being marked by a dark-brown spot, which gives the fish an unusual appearance.

***Leporinus fasciatus* — Banded Leporinus**
This is a very attractive fish with its broad, alternating bands of black and yellow. It is widely distributed in South America, although there is some difference in shading according to the locality where it was collected. Small specimens tend to be delicate, but larger ones grow to 13 inches and are very hardy.

Family CALLICHTHYIDAE

One of the more common catfishes in the hobby is Corydoras arcuatus. *Like other members of the genus, it is a tireless cleaner, raking about in the gravel for edible tidbits. Photo by A. van den Nieuwenhuizen.*

Family CALLICHTHYIDAE

Armored Catfishes

This family is restricted in distribution to the northern two-thirds of South America. Characteristic of the family is the presence of heavy, overlapping plates. Bottom dwellers, the Callichthyidae have an adaptation permitting them to breathe atmospheric oxygen with which to supplement that absorbed through the action of the gills. By far the greatest number of species in the family are found in the genus *Corydoras*. These droll little fellows are usually known as dwarf catfishes because few of them attain a length greater than two and one-half to three inches. It is interesting to watch them dart to the surface and gulp in a mouthful of air. Unlike the anabantoids, whose breathing organ is located in the head, the Callichthyidae swallow the air and absorb the oxygen as it passes through the intestine. Because the Callichthyidae have been called "scavengers" and frequent the bottom layer of the aquarium, it does not mean that they do not require careful feeding. No catfish can eat droppings or waste matter from other fishes; in fact, they create their own. Their value as scavengers lies in the fact that they grub ceaselessly over the bottom, searching for those bits of food overlooked and uneaten by other fishes which, if left to rot, would provide a focal point for contamination of the aquarium. Two *Corydoras* should be kept to each five gallons of aquarium water. They will, by digging actively into the upper layers of the gravel, even root out and remove Tubifex worms which have established themselves. These hide in the gravel and cannot be reached by most fishes.

A word of caution when handling catfishes: the leading spine of the dorsal and pectoral fins is extremely rigid, sharp and strong. The fish can erect and lock these fins into place, and a jab from one of them can be quite painful, the pain persisting out of all proportion to the extent of the puncture.

Most *Corydoras* are easily bred in the aquarium. After a characteristic dance, the male embraces the female, who then places several large eggs against a flat surface such as the aquarium glass or a rock. While apparently there is no parental care, the adults do not destroy their eggs unless hungry. The eggs hatch in five to eight days at an average temperature of 70°F.

Albino varieties of *Corydoras aeneus,* the Bronze Corydoras and *Corydoras paleatus,* the Peppered Corydoras, have been developed and are frequently available to aquarists.

Corydoras aeneus — **Bronze Corydoras**

This is a plain, greenish-bronze *Corydoras,* and one of the hardiest of its genus.

Corydoras arcuatus — **Skunk Corydoras**

One of the prettiest of the *Corydoras.* The body is clear-ivory varying to light beige in some specimens, but the distinctive mark is a black band which begins at the tip of the head and follows the arch of the back to the root of the tail. Here, it joins a transverse bar on the caudal peduncle and then continues along the lower edge of the tail. It is reported to be somewhat more delicate than other members of the genus.

Corydoras julii — **Leopard Corydoras**

This species derives its popular name both from its markings and from its former scientific name of *Corydoras leopardus.* The body color is a light silvery-gray varying

Brochis splendens

Corydoras aeneus

Bottom: Two hardy scavengers for the aquarium are Corydoras melanistius *(upper fish) and* C. julii *(lower fish). Photo by B. Kahl.*

to lavender; the tail is barred. There is a stripe consisting of a series of dots along the lateral line, numerous small dark dots all over the body and head, and a prominent dark tip to the dorsal fin.

Corydoras melanistius — Black-spotted Corydoras
Superficially, this fish resembles

The Glassfish Chanda ranga is a brackish species that requires some salt in its water. Adult males are quite lovely, with a blue edging to the dorsal and anal fins.

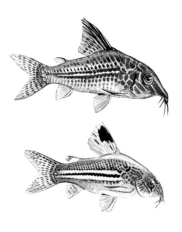

Top: Corydoras agassizi.
Bottom: Corydoras trilineatus.

the Leopard Corydoras. However, it may be distinguished by the following: the dorsal fin is more triangular and does not have the black tip, there is a black blotch on the body just below the forward edge of the dorsal fin, and a black vertical bar covers the head, commencing just behind the mouth and reaching upward through the eye, ending in a point at the edge of the dorsal.

Corydoras metae — Bandit Catfish or Masked Corydoras
More chunky than most Corydoras, the Bandit Catfish resembles arcuatus in ground

coloring. However, the stripe which on arcuatus follows the line of the back, extends only from the base of the tail to the dorsal fin in the metae. In addition, there is a vertical bar across the head through the eyes, giving it its popular name.

Corydoras punctatus — Spotted Corydoras
Superficially, this fish resembles the Leopard Catfish and the Blackspotted Corydoras. However, the spot markings on punctatus are much larger.

Hoplosternum thoracatum — Hoplo Cat
Heavily armored, Hoplosternum is found throughout the Amazon Basin and northern South

They are rather drab in color, a dark olive-brown with a lighter stomach, the young being covered with numerous black dots which make them quite attractive. As the young grow, the dots rearrange themselves so that they finally appear as narrow bands on the adult.

Family CENTROPOMIDAE

Glassfishes
While there are several glassfishes known to science, only one of this family is commonly seen in the aquarium, and that is *Chanda ranga*, or Indian Glassfish. A slow-moving, gentle fish, it has struck the imagination of aquarists and writers with its transparent glasslike body. In spite of this apparent delicacy, it is quite hardy. The males seem to reflect

America. Hoplo Cats, as they are commonly known, reach a length of seven to eight inches in nature, but seldom attain that length in the aquarium. Usually, they breed when between three to four inches. They are bubble nest builders, the male caring for the eggs and young.

Astyanax fasciatus is the normal form of the species, from which arose the subspecies mexicanum, *the Blind Cave Tetra. Photos by H. J. Richter.*

the light with a gold-to-orange-to-purple hue, making them quite attractive.

Family CHARACIDAE

The Characins

From the point of view of variety, the characins contribute the greatest number of species to our aquarium, varying from the lovely and peaceful Neon Tetra to the vicious Piranha. Most characins are found in South America, where they range south almost to the tip and northwards through Central America up into Mexico and Texas. A few characins are also found in Africa.

Many of the characins are similar in appearance to barbs, but no characins possess the barbels, which are fleshy appendages around the mouth. Most, but not all characins have a small fin called an **adipose fin** between the dorsal and caudal.

The Blind Cave Tetra, Astyanax fasciatus mexicanus, *gets around quite well in the aquarium in spite of its eyelessness. It has an excellent sense of smell and a highly developed lateral line system.*

For the most part, Characins prefer extremely soft, acid water. While they will tolerate quite a variation in water conditions, they will show their best colors and breed most freely when the pH is below 6.5 and the hardness in the water less than two to three degrees.

Most of the Characins are typical egg scatterers with no parental care being assumed. For the most part, they prefer living in groups, rather than pairs, and tend to be carnivorous.

Bloodfin Tetra
Aphyocharax anisitsi
Photo by Dr. Herbert R. Axelrod

While it is impossible to list all of them here, the most desirable Characins are as follows:

Astyanax fasciatus mexicanum — Blind Cave Tetra

This is one of the oddities of the fish world. It has spent so many hundreds or perhaps thousands of generations in lightless caves of Mexico that the eyes have atrophied and it can no longer see. The fish itself is a light pink and rather attractive. In spite of the "handicap" of blindness, the fish seems to find its way about the aquarium quite well, seldom bumping into obstacles.

Unfortunately, the Blind Cave Tetra has been known to nip fins and must be watched when left with smaller fishes.

Cardinal Tetra
Paracheirodon axelrodi
Photo by Dr. Herbert R. Axelrod

Neon Tetra
Paracheirodon innesi
Photo by A. Roth

Aphyocharax anisitsi — Bloodfin

This is another of the many small delightful Characins. Under good conditions the body gleams with a pearl to silver-white luster while the fins are deep blood red. This small fish, originally from Argentina, grows to about two inches in length. The parents are vigorous breeders, frequently leaping out of the water in their breeding frenzy.

Paracheirodon axelrodi — Cardinal Tetra

This delightful tetra from Brazil was introduced to aquarists in the 1950's, and closely resembles the Neon with its brilliant blue band above the red area. It is easy to distinguish between the two, however, because the red area covers the entire lower third of the Cardinal Tetra from the lower jaw to the tail. The red of the Neon begins about a quarter of

The long-finned form of the Black Tetra, Gymnocorymbus ternetzi. These fish are beautiful but tend to produce a percentage of deformed specimens when bred, so careful culling is necessary. Photo by A. Roth.

Hyphessobrycon flammeus

Hyphessobrycon erythrostigma

the way back at the pelvic fin, the forward area being white. In addition, the Cardinal is a larger, and especially when mature, heavier bodied fish. Like the Neon, it is an ideal aquarium fish, hardy and inoffensive.

Gymnocorymbus ternetzi —
Black Tetra
One might gain the impression from the name that this rather small Characin from the Mato Grosso on the Rio Negro is all black. Actually, only the anal fin can really be called black and this primarily is in younger fishes. The black fades to gray as the fish matures. There are also two black vertical bars on the forward part of the body and black hue throughout. The body is rounded although not quite so much so as is the Silver Dollar. The extremely long anal fin which runs from the vent to the tail is unusual for this type of small Characin. They breed when approximately one

and one-half inches in length. The colors of both sexes are similar, but the mature female is noticeably rounder.

Hemigrammus ocellifer —
Head-and-Tail-Light
Coming from the Amazon Basin in Guiana, this long-time favorite is likely to maintain its popularity for many years to come. The most noticeable features are the brilliant eyes (gold below, red above) and the shining spot on the caudal peduncle. These features give the fish its popular name. Viewed under a good light, one can see a fine, almost dotted white line running part way through the center of the anal fin of the male. Otherwise, the sexes may be distinguished by the more robust shape of the female.

Hemigrammus caudovittatus —
Buenos Aires Tetra
Originally collected from the Plate River near Buenos Aires, Argentina, the Buenos Aires Tetra is one of the oldest of aquarium fishes. However, aquarium-bred fishes lack much of the color of wild specimens. It grows fairly large, up to about three inches in length, and is known as a fin nipper and plant chewer. In spite of these drawbacks, it is still worth keeping, particularly with larger fishes, as it is hardy and attractive and requires no special conditions.

Hemigrammus erythrozonus —
Glowlight Tetra
This fish was originally collected in British Guiana and is truly one of the jewels of the aquarium world. Similar in shape to but slightly larger than the Neon, the outstanding feature is a golden band which runs from the gill cover to the base of the tail where it broadens out into a gleaming

spot. Apparently there are local color variations, as Glowlights collected in different areas of northern South America display varying shades of color ranging from a brassy-gold to a brilliant-red. Habits and care are similar to that required for the other small tetras. However, their breeding behavior is distinguished from similar fishes by the fact that the

Head-and-Tail-Light, but the Pulcher can grow to almost 2½ inches compared to the 1¾ inches of the Head-and-Tail-Light. Also, the "light" in the eye is not as prominent. There is a rectangular black patch on the caudal area, just below the golden spot.

Hemigrammus rhodostomus —

Top: *A breeding tank for tetras.* **Bottom:** *The Head-and-Tail Light Tetra,* Hemigrammus ocellifer.

male and female clasp fins and do a barrel roll while the eggs are being extruded. It grows to two inches. Its habitat is British Guiana.

Hemigrammus pulcher — Pulcher Tetra

Coming from the middle Amazon, the Pulcher is quite similar in shape and appearance to the

Rummy-nose Tetra

Coming from the lower Amazon, the Rummy Nose Tetra is instantly recognizable because its bright, red nose is exactly like the nose of a confirmed drunkard! The tail is striped, somewhat like that of the Scissortail Rasbora *(Rasbora trilineata);* although the lobes aren't as long, the black and white striping is more intense.

The Lemon Tetra, Hyphessobrycon pulchripinnis. *Photo by R. Zukal.*

The red coloration is present in both male and female, which are otherwise indistinguishable except for the shape. *H. rhodostomus* grows to about two inches, making it an ideal aquarium fish.

Hyphessobrycon flammeus — Tetra von Rio, or Flame Tetra

A long time favorite in the aquarium, and deservedly so, this rather small, 1½- to 2-inch fish is ideal in all respects. Like many characins, it tends to lose color when crowded or disturbed.

However, in soft, acid water and well-fed, particularly with live food, it fairly glows with a bright reddish-orange color from which it derives the nickname Flame Tetra. The ventral and anal fins of the male are bordered in black. Very hardy and easily bred, its habitat is the vicinity of Rio de Janeiro.

Paracheirodon innesi — Neon Tetra

This is a rather small fish which is adult when approximately 1½ inches in length. Like most

One of the Rummy-nose Tetras, Hemigrammus rhodostomus. *Photo by H. J. Richter.*

characins it prefers a temperature of 70° to 80°F. The Neon Tetra derives its name from the brilliant blue-green band of iridescent color running along the mid-section. This line is not actually fluorescent as it has no internal light of its own, but shines by reflecting overhead light. In the dark, this line fades to white, and the red area below which extends from the pelvic fin to the tail fades

Hyphessobrycon pulchripinnis — **Lemon Tetra**

The Lemon Tetra was imported from South America many years ago, and has proved so adaptable and breeds so freely in captivity that for many years no one has bothered to import wild specimens. Like the Tetra von Rio, the Lemon Tetra is one of those fishes which requires favorable conditions before it will

The Buenos Aires Tetra, Hemigrammus caudovittatus, *may be a fin nipper. Photo by Dr. Herbert R. Axelrod.*

to a pale pink. The color is regained shortly after the lights are turned on. The Neon is an extremely peaceful fish, but should not be kept with fishes large enough to swallow it. Breeding is difficult and seldom accomplished. However, success can be achieved by using extremely soft, acid water. It hails from Brazil.

display its delicate and lovely lemon-yellow and black coloration.

One of the outstanding features is its large eyes, the upper half of which are a bright red. The anal fin of the male is decorated with a broad black margin. The Lemon Tetra grows to about 2 inches.

Hyphessobrycon erythrostigma — **Bleeding Heart Tetra**

Imported in the 1950's, the

Bleeding Heart is similar in shape to the Serpae Tetra. However, it does grow considerably larger, up to three inches; it is also distinguishable from the Serpae by the prominent red marking on the shoulder which gives it its name. Because it is so much larger than the Serpae, an adult Bleeding Heart Tetra may be kept in a mixed community tank of larger fishes. The coloration of the male and female is identical; sexing is done by the differences in the dorsal and anal fin shapes. In the male these are elongated and pointed.

Like most Tetras, Hemigrammus pulcher *is best kept in schools. Photo by B. Kahl.*

Moenkhausia sanctaefilomenae is a large tetra that exceeds four inches in length. It is a long-lived species if well cared for, and specimens have been known to live for over a decade! Photo by J. Elias.

Moenkhausia sanctaefilomenae — Redeye Tetra

This medium-sized characin (up to four and one-half inches in length) is notable particularly for the brilliant eye coloring (which is red above and gold below) and from which the name is derived. The Redeye Tetra is extremely hardy and breeds readily.

Silver Dollars

These are a number of genera of

The Congo Tetra, Phenacogrammus interruptus, *is very delicately colored; its hues show best when the tank is diffusely lit.*

disc-shaped characins, primarily silver in color, from which they derive their popular name.

Superficially, the Silver Dollars resemble the Piranha because of their ovate shape. However, they may be easily distinguished from their bloodthirsty cousin because they lack the heavy lower jaw of the Piranha. The principal genera and their distinguishing features are as follows:

Metynnis: This is the largest genus, containing about twenty-two species. The adipose fin is

Phenacogrammus interruptus — Congo Tetra

This is the African characin most commonly imported and offered for sale.

It is a medium-sized (to about 3 inches) fish, commonly found throughout the Zaire Basin. Unfortunately, the smaller specimens lack the delicate green-gold of the adult. Given soft, acid water and an ample supply of live or high-protein food, it will bloom and reveal itself as one of the most beautiful of our aquarium fishes. The male is

The hot-pink stripe of the Glowlight Tetra, Hemigrammus erythrozonus, makes it one of the most beautiful Tetras. Photo by B. Kahl.

more elongated than that of the other Silver Dollars.

Myleus: The anal fin of *Myleus* is elongated, forming a distinctive sickle shape. The adipose is small, the dorsal elongated.

Mylossoma: The anal fin is rounded, the outer edge forming almost a half-moon shape; the adipose fin is small.

particularly beautiful, with pronounced coloring and elongated dorsal fin. The center rays of the male's tail also extend to form a spike.

Piranha

There are several genera, notably *Serrasalmus.* These are all deep-bodied, sturdy, bulldog-headed

Pristella
Pristella maxillaris
Photo by S. Frank

fishes whose jaws contain rows of triangular deltoid teeth. These sharp teeth are set in powerful jaws, enabling the Piranha to shear flesh away with a bite. Traveling in large schools as they do, they are an ever-present danger in the rivers and streams of tropical South America. Most aquarists familiar only with the small specimens usually imported are unaware that some species will grow to eighteen inches in length and several pounds in weight. At this size they really can be dangerous. Even small specimens are quite capable of giving a painful and bloody nip. Several people who have been bitten by Piranhas have reported to the author that they felt no more than a shock at the moment; it was only after they saw the blood that they realized that they had been bitten. In an aquarium, a Piranha is a rather dull and uninteresting fish. Surprisingly enough it tends to be timid. Foreign objects introduced into the aquarium such as a net or ornament frequently send it into a panic. It is at such times that a Piranha can be dangerous, as it will frantically bite at anything. It is also dangerous

because the degree of tameness which it acquires may cause the owner to become careless. Then one day, perhaps while feeding his fish, he trails his finger in the water only to lose a tip as the Piranha rises to the lure.

Needless to say, the Piranha had best be kept one to a tank. Small specimens may be fed the standard live foods, while the larger fishes will eat strips of meat and fish. Very little is known about their breeding habits.

Pristella maxillaris—Pristella

This is a fish which, in spite of the fact that it does not have particularly bright colors, is so neat and nicely put together that it is very pleasant to keep. In addition, it is easily bred and quite hardy. Originally imported from British Guiana, the Pristella tetra grows to approximately two inches. There is also an albino version with faint gold stripes on the dorsal fin and brilliant red eyes. Habitat: British Guiana.

The Penguin Tetra, Thayeria boehlkei, *swims with a characteristic tail-down posture.*

This Piranha, Serrasalmus *sp.*, shows the impressive dentition for which these characoids are famous. Although piranhas certainly do consume flesh, they also eat a great deal of vegetable matter and should be given some soft plants such as Elodea. For the meaty portion of their diet, feeder fish (goldfish and guppies) and crustaceans such as krill or shrimp are relished.

Thayeria boehlkei — Penguin Fish

Like some pencilfishes, these too swim at a tail-down forty-five degree angle. Unlike the pencilfishes, however, which tend to be slow moving, the Penguins are alert fishes which actively dart about in the water. When alarmed, they will assume a normal swimming posture and move rapidly. They do not breed particularly readily in the aquarium. However, if conditions are ideal they will reproduce. They are from the Amazon basin.

Family CICHLIDAE

Cichlids

The amount of interest shown in cichlids by students of animal behavior, correctly known as ethologists, and the amount of space devoted to cichlids in aquarium magazines and other publications devoted to fishes is justified because so many species are kept in aquaria. Many cichlids grow large and some are known as pugnacious plant destroyers. And yet, one cannot criticize this aspect of their behavior, for this is part of their pattern of living and breeding which makes them such interesting subjects for observation and study.

There are two notable exceptions to the generally pugnacious behavior of the larger cichlids, and these are the genera *Symphysodon,* commonly known as Discus, and *Pterophyllum,* or Angelfish. In general, the breeding behavior of these two follows the pattern of the majority of cichlids, which may be briefly described as follows: usually a male cichlid will set up a territory; that is, an area of the tank which is out of bounds to all other members of his species, although some types will tolerate other species of fishes swimming by. In extremely large aquaria, this territory may take up only a certain portion, and several male cichlids may establish territories within the confines of the single aquarium. However, in smaller tanks up to perhaps fifty gallons, it is usual for one male to assert himself as master of the entire area. If several males are introduced they will fight each other until one male dominates all, perhaps bullying the others to death. A strange fish approaching the borders of this territory, or introduced to the territory, is greeted by the dominant male whose behavior pattern is characteristic for that species. By the response of the newcomer, the occupant determines whether it is a male which should be attacked, or a female which should be courted. Should it be the latter, a series of signals is given which, if she gives the proper responses, culminates in mating. The signals are characterized by side to side wagging, tailflapping, and locking of the lips in what appears to be a wrestling bout. Preliminaries over, the two proceed to clear an area, usually a large, flat rock, cleaning it carefully with their thick rubbery lips to provide a place for the eggs to be laid and fertilized. Angelfish and Discus follow this pattern in general, preferring however, to lay their eggs on a vertical surface, frequently a plant leaf, rather than on a horizontal surface.

Both parents stand guard over the eggs, cleaning them with their lips and fanning them with their large pectoral fins. The young are guarded and attended to. The dwarf cichlids deviate only slightly from this procedure. They prefer a more sheltered area, such as an overturned flower pot or a cave formed from a rock, in which to deposit their eggs; the eggs may be deposited on either the bottom, the side, or the surface. Frequently, dwarf cichlids will burrow under a rock, laboriously removing the gravel grain by grain, until they have excavated a cavern deep enough to hide themselves. The female dwarf cichlid is more plainly colored and much smaller than the male; frequently though not invariably, the female alone cares for the eggs. This is not usually true of the larger cichlids, where both parents care for the family.

A *Zebra Angelfish. Many varieties of* Pterophyllum scalare *are now available thanks to selective breeding. Photo by H. J. Richter.*

in the sand into which the eggs are deposited. These are taken up in the mouth of one of the parents after being laid and fertilized. Which parent serves as a living incubator depends upon the species. The eggs, and subsequently the young, are carried in the mouth until they are free-swimming. In some species, the young may continue to use the mouth as a sanctuary for several days after they have emerged, returning there at the first sign of danger.

For the purposes of the aquarist, we will arbitrarily divide the cichlids into two groups by size, as follows:

Larger Cichlids
Aequidens maroni — Keyhole Cichlid
Aequidens portalegrensis — Porthole Acara
Astronotus ocellatus — Oscar
Cichlasoma octofasciatum — Jack Dempsey
Cichlasoma festivum — Flag Cichlid or Festivum
Cichlasoma meeki — Firemouth Cichlid
Cichlasoma nigrofasciatum — Convict Cichlid

Top: *A Red Devil,* Cichlasoma labiatum, *caring for its fry. Photo by Rainer Stawikowski.*
Right: *The Port Cichlid,* Aequidens portalegrensis, is somber-colored but is very easy to breed and thus a popular fish. Photo by R. Zukal.

The young, when free-swimming, are quite large and need not be fed infusoria at their first stage, but can be started directly on newly hatched brine shrimp and microworms.

One interesting group of cichlids is the mouthbrooders. These will excavate a small hollow

Convict Cichlid
Cichlasoma nigrofasciatum

Pink Convict Cichlid
Cichlasoma nigrofasciatum

Cichlasoma severum — Severum

Small Cichlids

Microgeophagus ramirezi — Ramirez' Dwarf Cichlid, or Ramirezi
Apistogramma pertense — Yellow Dwarf Cichlid
Apistogramma ortmanni — Ortmann's Dwarf Cichlid
Nannacara anomala — Golden Dwarf Cichlid

Also among this group of dwarf cichlids, none of which grow to more than three inches, we should include *Aequidens curviceps*. While somewhat larger than most dwarf cichlids (it may reach a length of 3½ inches) and deeper-bodied than most, it is a gentle, easily kept fish which is

not belligerent and does not destroy plants.

Vertical Spawners

Science divided the genus *Pterophyllum* into two species: *dumerilii* and *scalare.* However, to the amateur hobbyist they are all known as Angelfish, because they all resemble each other markedly in shape and finnage. The larger species is *scalare,* which reaches a vertical height of almost ten inches; *dumerilii* between eight and nine inches.

Angelfish have appeared in a number of color variations from the original silver fish with black vertical bands. Today, we have a dark hued Angelfish known as a "black lace" angel, an all-black form known appropriately as the black Angelfish, and a gold variety. In addition, there is an all silver type which has only faint indications of the bars and is known as a "ghost" angel. There is also a "blushing" Angelfish which has a ruddy area in the anterior portion of its body. In addition, the fins on the color varieties have been extended through selective breeding to form what is known as the "veiltail" Angelfish.

Usually a strip of slate is provided in an otherwise bare tank to receive the spawn. This is removed to a hatching tank when the eggs have been laid. An airstone which produces a fine bubble is set alongside the strip so that the current almost, but not quite, brushes the eggs. The young start to hatch in about 72 hours but cling in long wriggling strings to the slate. When they become free-swimming, feed them brine shrimp nauplii and similar-sized foods.

The other group of vertical spawners is the Discus. The two species considered valid by ichthyologists are *Symphysodon aequifasciata* and *Symphysodon discus*, although subspecies of both sometimes confuse the issue.

In its breeding, Discus

Top: A male Dwarf Egyptian Mouthbrooder, Pseudocrenila-brus multicolor. Photo by H. J. Richter. *Left:* The stately Discus is among the most prized of aquarium fishes. This fish is shy and is not good in a community tank, preferring the sedate company of its own kind. Photo by G. Marcuse. *Right:* Two common dwarf cichlids, Nannacara anomala *(top)* and Microgeophagus ramirezi *(bottom).*

superficially resembles *Pterophyllum.* That is, they spawn on a vertical surface, either a strip of slate or broad-leaf plant, and both parents care for the young. The major difference is that the young Discus, upon becoming free-swimming, feed on a substance secreted in the skin cells of the parents. This has been analyzed as a combination of proteins and fats exuded at the surface of the epidermis. After several days of being "nursed,"

the young assume more normal eating habits and will thrive on a diet of newly-hatched brine shrimp, sifted daphnia, microworms, and so on. Because of the apparent necessity for obtaining their "first foods" from the parents, the eggs cannot be removed for separate hatching as can be done with most other cichlids.

The Discus, and we use the name Discus to include all the various species or subspecies,

breed much less freely than do the Angelfish. The majority of Angelfish seen in our aquaria are tank-raised, whereas the overwhelming majority of Discus are still imported.

Like most cichlids, Discus prefer live food as a regular basic diet. In fact, it is probably mandatory if breeding is to be attempted. Extremely soft, aged, somewhat acidic water is preferred.

African Cichlids

In recent years the aquarium hobby has been taken by storm by a plethora of interesting cichlids from Lakes Malawi and Tanganyika in Africa's Rift Valley. The popularity of these fishes is in part due to their hardiness and ease of breeding, but mostly because many are extremely colorful.

The most available fishes from Lake Tanganyika are the various species of *Lamprologus* and *Julidochromis*. In general, these are sleek, torpedo-shaped substrate spawners. They are somewhat secretive and like a great deal of rockwork in their tank in which they will lurk and

Kuhli Loaches such as Acanthophthalmus myersi *are secretive fishes that need a well-covered aquarium to prevent their escape. Photo by Dr. Herbert R. Axelrod.*

later spawn. The Tanganyikan substrate-spawners are mostly carnivorous and enjoy live brine shrimp and bloodworms.

From Lake Malawi come the stunning mbuna. They are usually bright-colored and not nearly so secretive as the Tanganyikans, although they too appreciate rocky shelter. Though they will accept all foods with gusto, they are primarily plant-eaters, rasping algae from rocks. All are mouthbrooders.

Both groups of Africans are aggressive fishes, especially when breeding. In aquaria, it is best to maintain them in a "controlled crowding" situation—in a large community there is less chance of a single fish being attacked relentlessly. However, it goes without saying that in such a setup attention to water quality is vital, and most African cichlids enjoy frequent partial water changes.

Family COBITIDAE

Loaches and Spined Loaches

Found throughout Europe, Asia and Africa, loaches are all bottom-dwelling fishes. They vary from the worm-like *Acanthophthalmus* to the shark-like *Botia*. The term "shark-like," as used for the *Botia*, refers to the wedge-like shape, high dorsal fin and underslung mouth, and not to their habits, which are usually gentle and retiring.

Even those loaches which are not worm-shaped have inferior mouths, well adapted for rooting from the bottom. Many of the loaches are nocturnal, spending the day hidden in the plants. For these species, cover in the form of an inverted half-coconut shell, a flowerpot, or a rock cave should be provided. Many loaches dive headlong into the gravel and with a series of wriggles bury themselves completely when disturbed.

Loaches seem to be responsive to changes in the atmospheric pressure, responding with increased activity. This

Botia sidthimunki

Misgurnus anguillicaudatus

characteristic is notable particularly in the Japanese Weatherfish *(Misgurnus anguillicaudatus)* of Japan and China. The loaches have been used as scavengers because of their bottom-feeding habits. However, for this purpose *Corydoras* are unquestionably superior. The sexes of loaches

The Skunk Loach, Botia morleti. *Photo by K. Paysan.*

Botia macracantha, *the ever-popular Clown Loach. Photo by Dr. K. Knaack.*

are difficult to distinguish, and there is very little report of their breeding activity in the aquarium. Certain genera are active algae eaters.

Acanthophthalmus — Coolie (Kuhli) Loaches
There are several species of the genus *Acanthophthalmus,* all of which have been imported and sold interchangeably under the name "coolie." The two commonest are *A. kuhlii* and *A. myersi.* Both are pinkish and dark-brown banded, but *myersi* is slimmer and has fewer bands. These are worm-like loaches with bristly whiskers about their soft, underslung mouths. Reaching the length of more than three inches, their slender shape makes them easy prey for vicious fishes. They, however, can be kept safely with other small aquarium inhabitants. As they are strictly bottom dwellers, care should be taken to see that adequate food reaches their feeding area.

Genus *Botia*
A number of members of this genus have been imported for use as aquarium fishes. However, only a few of them are really attractive and worth considering. *Botia* are similar in shape to the *Labeo,* but may possess a cheek spine. This spine, which is found wholly or partly developed in a number of the genera of the loach family, is a bony spike located between the nose and eye of the fish and slightly below the level of the eye. Normally, these spikes are folded and barely visible; however, they can be, and are, erected voluntarily by the fish in the presence of danger and lock in position with often disastrous consequences for the predator attempting to, or succeeding in, swallowing the loach.

The following *Botia* are the most generally available aquarium inhabitants:

Botia morleti—Skunk Botia
From Thailand, this primarily yellowish-green to pale brick-colored fish can reach a length of almost four inches. The distinctive markings are a black stripe along the back, from the snout to the tail, continuing as a comma-shaped marking on the caudal peduncle.

Botia hymenophysa. *Photo by M. Gilroy.*

Botia modesta. *Photo by K. Knaack.*

Botia macracantha — Clown Loach

This, the most beautiful and only really popular species of *Botia,* is found in Sumatra and Borneo. While the shape is typically *Botia,* the coloration reminds one of the Tiger Barb; alternating deep black and ivory-colored bands with bright red fins and tail. In common with most *Botia* species as well, in fact, as with most bottom-dwelling fishes, they are very susceptible to infestations of Ich. This is because during one stage of the life cycle of that parasite the mature parasite drops off the whole fish, and multiplies on the bottom. When the cyst bursts, releasing the free-swimming stage of the parasites, they of course encounter the bottom-dwelling fishes first and attack them. Coupled with this is the fact that many *Botia* species tend to hide. Therefore, it is necessary to examine them regularly for signs of infestations so that treatment may be started before the disease has reached a serious phase.

Botia modesta — Blue Botia

There are two closely-related species, *Botia modesta* and *Botia pulchripinnis* (Red-finned Blue Botia). Both of them have a blue to pale-green body but, whereas the fins and tail of *modesta* tend to be yellow, *pulchripinnis* has bright orange to red fins. *B. modesta* is found from the Malay Peninsula to Thailand and grows to a length of almost four inches. While attractive, it will dig depressions in the sand and has been known to harass other fishes.

Botia sidthimunki — Dwarf Loach

The Dwarf Loach from Thailand reaches a length of 1½ to 2 inches. It is distinctively marked, and once seen not easily forgotten. A black line extends from the tip of the nose into the caudal peduncle, where it becomes a blotch. The stomach is white, the fins colorless except for a little yellow at the base of the tail and a few chocolate or dark gray marks near the margins of the lobe. Another black stripe extends from the nose through the eye and along the back, also ending at the blotch on the caudal peduncle. These center and upper bars are connected vertically with six irregularly shaped half bars. A rectangular-shaped yellow patch on the head is matched by five thumbprint-shaped yellow blotches between the vertical bars. Peaceful, gentle and somewhat retiring, the Dwarf Loach is an ideal aquarium fish.

Family CYPRINIDAE

Widely distributed throughout the world, the Cyprinidae are found in the United States, Mexico, and southern Canada, all of Africa, and Asia. There are about fifteen hundred species, many of which are desirable aquarium fishes. In fact, the well-known Goldfish (scientifically known as *Carassius auratus)* is a member of this family.

Balantiocheilus melanopterus — Tri-color Shark

There are a number of aquarium fishes which share the name "shark." Many of them are of different genera, even, in fact, of different families. Thus, they are not really closely related but bear the name in common because of resemblance in shape to their namesake.

The back of the Tri-color Shark is arched and there is a large, triangular dorsal fin. Its body is silvery or bluish-silver, but the fins give the fish its distinction. They are an intense yellow with deep-black margins. The fins are usually kept spread out in a sprightly manner. Found in Thailand, Borneo, and Sumatra, adults can attain a length of fourteen inches. However, young specimens are very desirable, hardy, and easily-fed.

Barbs

Representatives of this group are found throughout Asia and Africa and Europe. Like the characins, the barbs provide a large number of species of aquarium fishes. Most of them are large-scaled and hardy, while many, though not all, have the barbels or fleshy appendages on the mouth from which the name is derived.

The barbs do not have an adipose fin. The barbs are frequently split into four genera: *Barbus, Barbodes, Puntius,* and *Capoeta,* though some prefer to lump all barbs into *Barbus.*

Most of the small barbs prefer being kept in small schools of three to six individuals where they actively spend their time playing and darting through the plants.

An example of the eagerness

Gold Barb, Puntius *sp. cf.* sachsi. *Photo by H. J. Richter.*

with which they school is the manner in which one can empty a tank of all, or most of its barbs, in the following manner: a large net is held vertically, perpendicular to and with one edge against the front glass of the aquarium. By using a smaller net like a shepherd's crook, one can herd an entire school of barbs into the waiting net.

Typical of the adhesive egglayers, the male drives the female vigorously until, assuming a side-by-side position, the eggs are scattered through the plants.

Top: The Tri-color Shark, Balantocheilus melanopterus, *is an active fish that needs a lot of swimming room. Photo by J. Vierke.* **Bottom:** *Two male Rosy Barbs,* Puntius conchonius.

Capoeta titteya. *Photo by H. Hansen.*

Puntius conchonius — **Rosy Barb**

An extremely hardy, medium-sized barb, this species is likely to maintain its popularity for years to come. Ordinarily rather colorless, during breeding season the male turns a brilliant, almost raspberry red color which must be seen to be appreciated. It is easily bred in captivity and enjoys a varied diet, thriving on either live or dried food. The dorsal fin of the male has a black tip which is lacking in the female. Like so many other of the popular barbs, the Rosy Barb comes from northern India and grows to a length of two and one-half inches.

Barbodes everetti — Clown Barb

Found in Singapore and nearby Borneo, the Clown Barb reaches a length of more than five inches. In spite of its large size, it is a relatively peaceful barb and can be trusted with all but the tiniest species. The name "clown" is due to the large, blue-green splotches like the polka dots of the circus clown. The fins of the male are bright orange, much paler in the female.

Puntius nigrofasciatus — Black Ruby

Originally imported from Ceylon, this smallish, 2 to 2½ inch barb is one of the ideal aquarium fishes. Ordinarily an ivory-colored fish with three to four blackish vertical bars, the color changes dramatically during the breeding season. Then the male is suffused with a purple-red glow particularly brilliant in the head region. The entire fish sparkles with a jewel-like luster. The dorsal fin of the male is solid black, while that of the female is almost colorless.

Capoeta oligolepis — Checkered Barb

This lovely little barb, originally from Sumatra, rarely reaches a

length of two inches. However, with its bluish-black, checkerboard marked sides and bright orange fins, it is a living gem. Peaceful, hardy, and easily fed, *oligolepis* may be kept in any mixed collection of small fishes. The vertical fins of the male are black-bordered and much more brightly colored than are those of the female.

Puntius sachsi — Gold Barb

Coming from Singapore and the Malayan Peninsula, this smallish barb, up to three inches in length, is distinctive with its bright golden color. There are probably several closely related strains or subspecies, as the color in different specimens varies in intensity from a pale yellow to a bright orange. This color seems unrelated to the conditions under which they are kept and the various color phases breed true.

Barbodes schwanenfeldi — Tinfoil Barb

This barb reached us via Thailand although it is said to be found also in Sumatra, Borneo, and Malacca. A rather large barb, reaching a length of over fourteen inches, young specimens with their brilliant, silvery sides flashing are very attractive in the aquarium. The dorsal and tail are bright red, the dorsal is black-tipped, and the forks of the tail are each defined with a black bar.

The specimens which reach our aquarium are, for the most part, collected in the wild, as there are very few records of this fish breeding in captivity, and the large size at which it matures would preclude the probability that the average aquarist has the tank capacity to encourage breeding. Young specimens should be provided with ample swimming room. They are also heavy feeders and, fortunately, will eat a variety of food.

Puntius tetrazona tetrazona — Tiger Barb

One of the most conspicuous and desirable of the barbs, this little fellow from Sumatra, Borneo, and Thailand can reach a length of

Clown Barb
Barbodes everetti
Photo by Dr. Herbert R. Axelrod

Tinfoil Barb
Barbodes schwanenfeldi
Photo by K. Paysan

Checker Barb
Capoeta oligolepis
Photo by A. Roth

almost three inches. A deep-bodied barb, the black and ivory-striped sides with their sharply defined bars and the bright red rims waving merrily as the fish sports actively about is a pretty sight to see. This fish has often been accused, unjustly in the opinion of the author, of being a fin-nipper, although it is probable that fin nipping does occur when the fishes are kept singly or in pairs. This may be due to the strong schooling instinct of the

***Capoeta titteya* — Cherry Barb**
Originally imported from Ceylon, this two-inch barb breeds so freely in captivity that all the specimens you see today are probably tank raised. The male, when in breeding condition, shows a brilliant raspberry-red hue which is extremely attractive. At other times, they are a rather dull-colored fish with pinkish-brown color and dull, dark red horizontal stripes. The female may be distinguished from the

The lovely Black Ruby Barb, Puntius nigrofasciatus. *Like most Barbs, it is an egg scatterer that is not fussy about foods or water conditions.*

barb, which can be best satisfied by keeping them in groups of four or more. The Tiger Barb is extremely hardy and breeds freely in typical egg-scatterer manner. The dorsal fin of the male is edged with a broad red band with the balance being black. The coloring of the female's dorsal is not nearly as intense, but she shows a narrow clear band between the black and the red.

male when not in breeding color by the deeper chest and body area.

Genera *Danio* and *Brachydanio*
Found throughout the Indian subcontinent, as well as in nearby areas, these fishes, which are all commonly known as "danios," are slim, colorful and active. They include the well-known Zebra Danio *(Brachydanio rerio)* and the

Pearl Danio (*Brachydanio albolineatus*).

The Giant Danio (*Danio malabaricus*) grows to almost five inches in length, whereas the *Brachydanio* species mentioned above seldom exceed two inches. In an aquarium the danios are constantly in movement flashing back and forth. Unlike most of the Cyprinidae they lay non-adhesive eggs. Breeding is accomplished in long, shallow tanks with the bottom liberally covered with material, such as marbles or fine plants, to hide the spawn. Spawning usually takes place in groups of three to five fishes with more males than females. Usually three males to two females is the most satisfactory proportion. Professional breeders use marbles as bottom cover, but *Myriophyllum* or some other fine-fronded plant may be weighted down with glass rods as a satisfactory spawning medium. The water literally seems to boil

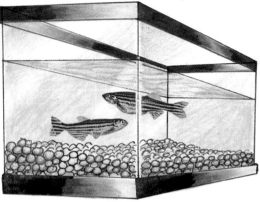

as the fishes race back and forth depositing their eggs. Spawning completed, the adults are removed and the young hatch in twenty to twenty-four hours. It takes them about twenty-four to thirty hours more to absorb their yolk sac, after which time they may be fed the finest of live food or finely ground dried food.

Labeo bicolor — Redtailed Black Shark

The deep, velvety black beauty which contrasts so strikingly with the blood-red tail must be seen to be appreciated. Imported in great numbers from Bangkok, Thailand, one of the great fish-shipping

Left: *A breeding tank for barbs and other cyprinids. The layer of marbles allows the eggs to fall beyond the reach of the hungry parents.* **Bottom:** *A spawning pair of Tiger Barbs,* Capoeta tetrazona. *Photo by H. J. Richter.*

ports of the world, the Redtailed Black Shark has found a ready market in America.

Today, because of the large numbers in which it has been imported, the price has come down dramatically, but it still remains a very desirable fish. This is not one of the larger "sharks," growing only to about 4½ inches in length. This fish feeds extensively on algae which it sucks up with its underslung mouth.

Morulius chrysophekadion — Black Shark

This fish is related to the Redtailed Black Shark, but the black is not as intense and it grows considerably larger, up to almost two feet. The Black Shark is found in Thailand. As specimens age, the intense color tends to fade with just a golden glint showing through. The black will also fade if the fish are kept in alkaline water or in an environment where they are being continually disturbed. These sharks love to browse on algae and will eat almost any fish food, live or prepared. The mouth is located underneath, somewhat like that of the suckers of the U.S.

Genus *Rasbora*

There are twenty-six or more species of the genus known to aquarists. However, the majority of them are rather plain-colored fish and even when available are not eagerly sought out. There are a few members of the genus, however, which because of their beauty, elegance, and general desirability should be included in this catalogue of those fishes most desirable for the home aquarium.

In general, *Rasbora* are schooling fishes and do best when kept in small groups of from

Rasbora heteromorpha—Harlequin Rasbora

three to four individuals, up to a dozen or more. With the exception of the Harlequin Rasbora *(Rasbora heteromorpha),* the members of this genus are all plant scatterers that lay their eggs more or less indiscriminately, and the eggs, being adhesive, attach themselves to the first object they touch. The rasboras do not spawn as freely as do some of the other fishes, such as the barbs, and, therefore, separate conditioning of the sexes for a period of ten days should precede the actual bringing together of the breeders.

Rasboras, which in general come from clear, flowing streams, should have ample swimming room in acid, aged, soft water. They do not display the hurried activity of some fishes such as the danios, but neither are they lethargic. They swim sedately and daintily about the mid-region of the tank in a characteristic "flashing fins" manner.

Black Shark
Morulius chrysophekadion
Photo by A. Kochetov

Sexing the Harlequin Rasbora is difficult for the inexperienced. Close observation will reveal that in addition to the usual differences in body shape, the female being more rounded and heavier, the forward lower corner of the blue-black triangle is pointed and complete in the male, whereas the same corner or angle in the female is rounded.

The water for breeding the Red Rasbora should be about 80°F, extremely soft and acidic, a pH of 5.3 being recorded by some

Labeo bicolor *is the Red-tailed Black Shark. As the fish grows, the body becomes a deep velvety black, the tail a brilliant scarlet. Photo by B. Walker.*

Rasbora heteromorpha — Harlequin Rasbora
This, the most popular of the rasboras, has been imported from the Far East in great numbers.

successful aquarists. Actual spawning takes place with the pair side-by-side in an upside-down position beneath the underside of a broad-leafed plant such as a *Cryptocoryne,* or

Brachydanio rerio

Amazon Swordplant *(Echinodorus)*. The eggs are pale amber in color and ignored by the parents. It is also reported that the parents do not eat their own young.

Rasbora maculata — Spotted Rasbora or Pigmy Rasbora

This is one of our smallest egglayers, adults barely reaching a length of one inch. Imported from the southern Malay Peninsula and Sumatra, the Pigmy Rasbora is quite pretty with clown-like blotches near the head, anal, posterior portion, and at the base of the tail. An overall glow when the fish is in good condition distinguishes this species. Because of its small size, the Pygmy Rasbora had best be kept only with the smallest and

Brachydanio albolineatus

Danio aequipinnatus

Rasbora heteromorpha "hengeli"

Rasbora kalochroma

Rasbora trilineata

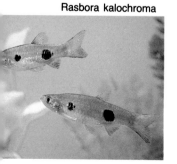

gentlest fishes, such as Neons and Glowlights. However, they will do quite well in a baby-rearing tank, enjoying the small-sized food which is fed to the babies and ignoring their tank-mates.

Rasbora pauciperforata — Redlined Rasbora

This lovely Rasbora is somewhat similar in appearance to the Glowlight Tetra because it too has a red stripe running horizontally along the mid-section. The Redlined Rasbora, which comes from Sumatra, is larger than the Glowlight, attaining the length of 2¾ inches. In addition, the outline is much slimmer and the line tends to a copper or fiery red rather than the paler golden glow of the Glowlight Tetra. Both sexes are identical in markings, sex being distinguished by the shape.

Redlined Rasbora, Rasbora pauciperforata.

Long-finned White Cloud Tanichthys albonubes Photo by H. J. Richter

This is a female Harlequin Rasbora, as evidenced by its extremely robust profile. Photo by J. Elias.

Rasbora trilineata — Scissortail Rasbora

This fish has no gaudy colors, does not have an odd or unusual shape, and does not have any unique habits to recommend it. Yet, year after year, it maintains its popularity solely because of its quiet, pleasing manners and neat yet elegant markings. The most outstanding feature of this fish is the distinctive tail markings from which it derives its name. The tail is deeply forked, with the two lobes extended and somewhat rounded. There are two prominent white spots on each lobe, with a distinct black blotch or bar between. As the fish swims, it flicks the lobes open and closed, giving a scissoring impression; otherwise, the fish is predominantly silver. It breeds freely in typical egg-scatterer fashion, and is hardy and gentle. The sexes are identical in color and markings, distinguished only by the greater girth of the female.

Tanichthys albonubes — White Cloud Mountain Minnow

Actually, this is a temperate zone fish from near Canton, China, and was collected in the White Mountains, hence its name. Easily bred in captivity, the iridescent stripe which is particularly bright in young specimens at one time caused this fish to be called "the poor man's Neon Tetra." A gentle, easily-fed fish, it can be kept in groups in a well-planted aquarium and will not eat the eggs or young when properly fed. The eggs are laid at intervals over a period of days, with the young being hatched at intervals also.

Family CYPRINODONTIDAE

Killifishes

The egg-laying Cyprinodontidae are extremely interesting and varied in coloration. The majority of them are long, slim, torpedo-like fishes, distributed throughout the temperate and tropical areas of the world, and in every continent of the world except Australia.

Most of the killifishes are slow-moving, sluggish fishes, usually inhabiting the upper areas of the aquarium. In this family are found some of the most highly colored

An Aphyosemion *species allied to* calliurum.

Red-chinned Epiplatys
Epiplatys dageti

Six-barred Epiplatys
Epiplatys sexfasciatus

of all our aquarium fishes. Where live food is not available, they easily may be trained to take frozen foods such as frozen brine shrimp and frozen daphnia. Small portions of these may be dropped into the rising stream of air from an aerator thus imparting motion to the particles.

For those people who specialize in killifishes (and there are thousands of them), the reward is well worth the effort. Many are beautiful and all are interesting to breed.

In breeding habits they can be divided into two groups: the plant spawners and the bottom spawners. Plant spawners lay their adhesive eggs, a few at a time, over a period of days on the fine-leafed fronds of such plants as *Myriophyllum* and hornwort. Commercial breeders use nylon mops and commercial spawning

media to receive the spawn. The tank is examined daily and the eggs removed into smaller containers. Usually, a new container is started every sixth day. These containers, which can be one-gallon jars, are kept in a dimly-lit area until the young hatch. The first few days are spent absorbing the egg yolk. The free-swimming young are large enough to be fed newly-hatched brine shrimp.

An aquarium with a layer of sand, peat moss, or nylon mop on the bottom is provided for the bottom spawners. These can be subdivided into two groups, those which corkscrew themselves down into the bottom, and those which lay their eggs just below the surface. Bottom spawners also lay their eggs over a period of time, rather than all in one spawning. After removal from the

Playfair's Panchax
Pachypanchax playfairi

Guenther's Notho
Nothobranchius guentheri

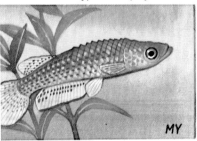

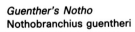

aquarium, the peat moss, if used, is kept moist in a plastic bag in a dimly-lit area. After two to four weeks, depending on the species, water is slowly added to the peat, and hatching usually takes place shortly thereafter.

Feeding is similar for both types: newly-hatched brine shrimp, microworms, and other fine foods. It is not necessary to feed infusoria. Growth is rapid, and the young should be separated according to size to prevent cannibalism. Because of the great number of killifishes, and as most of these are recommended only for the more

Aphyosemion sjoestedti — Golden Pheasant
Aplocheilus lineatus — Striped Panchax
Aplocheilus panchax — Blue Panchax
Cynolebias bellotti — Argentine Pearlfish
Cynolebias nigripinnis — Blackfinned Pearlfish
Micropanchax macrophthalmus — Lampeyed Panchax
Nothobranchius guentheri — Guenther's Notho
Nothobranchius rachovi — Rachov's Notho
Oryzias latipes — Medaka or

Silver Hatchetfish, Gasteropelecus sternicla. *Photo by B. Kahl.*

advanced aquarists, a detailed description is beyond the scope of this book, which is intended primarily for the beginner.

However, a list of those most available and most desirable is included for the benefit of those aquarists who would like to try their hand with these most interesting fishes.

Aphyosemion australe australe — Lyretail Panchax
Aphyosemion bivittatum bivittatum — Red Lyretail

Ricefish
Rivulus cylindraceus — Cuban Rivulus

Family GASTEROPELECIDAE

In this family, we find three genera of freshwater "flying fishes" commonly known to the aquarist as hatchetfishes. Primarily surface swimmers and surface feeders, the hatchetfishes are lovely, odd, and unusual aquarium inhabitants. They are extremely peaceful and somewhat

delicate unless kept in soft water and fed a small-sized food. Drosophila, or fruit flies, which are tiny and float on the surface, are an excellent addition to the diet of the hatchetfishes. Hatchetfishes should be kept away from bullying fishes, as they are relatively peaceful and defenseless. Motion pictures taken of the hatchetfishes show that as they leap from the water they beat their fins strongly, adding impetus to the leap or flight. For such tiny fishes (most less than two inches in length) to make flights of ten to fifteen feet is truly marvelous.

The three hatchetfishes most commonly kept in the aquarium are: *Carnegiella strigata,* commonly known as the Marbled Hatchetfish; *C. marthae,* the Blackwinged Hatchetfish; and *Gasteropelecus sternicla,* the Silver Hatchetfish. The Silver and the Blackwinged Hatchetfish are similar in coloration, but the Silver is much larger than these. It grows up to 2½ inches in length, while the tiny, glasslike Blackwinged Hatchetfish barely reaches 1½ inches. The Marbled Hatchetfish is between the two in size, about 1¾ inches.

Above: The Chinese Algae Eater, Gyrinocheilus aymonieri, *is an excellent cleaner of algae, but larger specimens are sometimes a bit pugnacious. Photo by H. J. Richter.* **Below:** *The most common species of* Carnegiella *in the hobby are* C. strigata *(large fish) and* C. marthae *(small fish). Photo by B. Kahl.*

Family GYRINOCHEILIDAE
Only one member of this family is of interest to the aquarist, and

Pencilfishes are very shy, so do not put them with fishes much larger than themselves. With their tiny mouths, they prefer small live foods such as bloodworms, tubifex, and brine shrimp. Photo of Nannostomus beckfordi by H. J. Richter.

that is the Chinese Algae Eater, *Gyrinocheilus aymonieri.* Actually, this fish should be called the Siamese or Thai Algae Eater, because it is widely distributed throughout Thailand. An elongated, gray-marked fish, the algae eater can attain a length of ten inches but rarely grows anywhere near this size in the aquarium.

Most Algae Eaters are imported as young specimens approximately two inches in length. They are quite inoffensive. Like animated vacuum cleaners, they move busily about the aquarium, ingesting algae which

Three-lined Pencilfish
Nannostomus trifasciatus
Photo by M. Youens

Nannostomus espei
Photo by H. J. Richter

they rasp off and inhale with their sucker-like mouths.

Both sexes are similar in markings and there are no reports of their having been bred in the aquarium.

Family LEBIASINIDAE

Pencilfishes

There are a number of important aquarium species in this group, included in the genera *Nannostomus* and *Nannobrycon*. All of these are slow-moving, small-mouthed, gentle fishes. They like a well-planted, brightly lit aquarium and seem to enjoy sunshine. Because of the small size of their mouths, they must be fed smaller-sized foods. Such live foods as Tubifex and white worms are best chopped or minced with a razor blade and rinsed before feeding. These fishes are all found in central and northern South America where they inhabit small, slow-moving streams.

One unusual characteristic is the dark vertical barring which appears when the fishes are kept in the dark or frightened. This may be seen when the aquarium lights are turned on after a period of darkness. This dark barring slowly fades away when light conditions return to normal. While the pencilfishes do not breed as freely as do some of the other aquarium egglayers, they will respond to conditioning in soft, acid, peat water. The eggs, which are scattered in fine leafed plants, are eaten voraciously by the parents as well as by any other fishes which are present, and should be removed as soon as possible. In addition to the broader outline of the female, sexing may be accomplished by studying the shape of the anal fin. The anal fin of the male is always rounded below. This is

particularly noticeable in those species which have white-edged fins such as *Nannostomus trifasciatus* (Three Banded Pencilfish).

All species mentioned, with the sole exception of *Nannostomus espei*, are striped longitudinally. *N. espei* is distinguished by four prominent, almost comma-shaped black blotches on the body. All are long slim fishes.

Family LORICARIIDAE

Heavily armored, the members of this family, distinguished by their sucker mouths, are commonly called "suckermouth" catfishes. Members of this family are useful as aquarium scavengers. Although they have a tendency to hide during the day, they are

Whiptailed Catfish
Rineloricaria cf. hasemani
Photo by A. Roth

Peppered Sucking Catfish
Otocinclus flexilis
Photo by Dr. Warren E. Burgess

Some people will insist that all loricariid catfishes are "ugly," but one look at this fish should be enough to prove the error of that statement. Pterygoplichthys gibbiceps *is spectacularly patterned, with an incredible sail-like dorsal fin. Like all loricariids, it requires large amounts of algae or other plant-based foods. Photo by A. Norman.*

active at night busily engaged in cleaning algae from the glass, rocks, and leaves of the plants. There are several genera in the group, and in the trade they are seldom distinguished by species. The genera *Ancistrus* and *Hypostomus* are roughly similar in shape: large heads tapering to a narrow tail, a fairly large dorsal fin which is erected often, heavy armoring, and an underslung mouth with which they cling to various objects. *Ancistrus,* however, have bristly snouts, that is, "whiskers" which may or may not be forked, protruding from the forward position of their head. Once seen, these are always recognizable, looking for all the world like pictures of the mythical Medusa. The various species of *Hypostomus* lack these bristles. All of these catfishes are excellent scavengers at the smaller sizes, i.e., up to about three inches.

Ancistrus dolichopterus, commonly known as the Bristlenose Catfish, reaches a length of up to 5½ inches. In addition to the bristles, there is a peculiar structure — a cluster of spines on either side of its head which can be erected when the fish is alarmed.

Hypostomus plecostomus (Pleco or Suckermouth), the most commonly imported of this group, may reach up to ten inches in length and sometimes grows to two feet.

All of the above are drab colored fishes, some with spots,

Twig Catfish
Farlowella species
Photo by H. J. Richter

and all are found in northern South America.

Farlowella gracilis — Twig Catfish

Here we see protective form and coloration to the greatest degree. Shaped for all the world like an old twig, the camouflage is further heightened by the dark-brown blotched coloration. The fins are transparent, the outer rays of the tail being extended as filaments.

Rineloricaria parva—Alligator Catfish

A long, slim, gray fish with dark

Among the few loricariids that have been spawned in aquaria are several Ancistrus *species. Photo by U. Werner.*

blotches from central South America, it reaches a length of five inches although most aquarium specimens seldom exceed three. It is heavily armored, the male being distinguished by the more pointed shape of its head.

Genus *Otocinclus*

These are smaller "sucker-mouths," seldom reaching more than two inches in length. The most commonly imported is *Otocinclus arnoldi,* which is usually imported from the southern region of Brazil between Rio de Janeiro and Manaus. Ideal as an algae cleaner, particularly in the smaller aquariums, they prefer being kept in groups and have been bred in the aquarium successfully.

Family MOCHOKIDAE

All the members of this catfish family come from Africa. As yet, not too many of them have been imported, but several are included here because it is probable that in the future, when collecting facilities and transportation from Africa to Europe and America improve, they will be arriving in increasing numbers.

The Mochokidae are largely schooling fishes which prefer dimly lit areas, avoiding bright light. In captivity, they will hide behind large plants, overhanging rocks, or flower pots; or if caves are provided, they can usually be found within. Dimming the lights of the aquarium will bring them out to view. They are peaceful and will thrive equally well on live or dried foods. All of the Mochokidae have three pairs of long barbels, some of which are branched or feathered.

Synodontis angelicus. *Photo by H. J. Richter.*

Synodontis schoutedeni. *Photo by H. J. Richter.*

Synodontis ornatipinnis. *Photo by H. J. Richter.*

Synodontis angelicus — Polkadot Catfish

One of the most attractive of the catfishes, the Polkadot Catfish derives its name from the numerous reddish-yellow to dark red spots scattered over its purple-gray body. These dots are larger on the head and the rear portion and extend onto the stomach area. First imported from the Congo, this fish can reach a length of eight inches. The young specimens are much more beautiful because the markings, which are white to light-yellow, stand out distinctly.

Synodontis nigriventris — Upside-down Catfish

Not particularly colorful, this catfish from the central Congo, which is mostly a mottled light and dark-brown or gray, is worth including in the aquarium collection because of its peculiar habit of swimming upon its back. Young Upside-down Catfish swim quite normally but as they mature, the swim bladder which enables a fish to maintain its level in the water gradually shifts position with the result that it is easier for the fish to swim upside-down than right side up. Normally, a fish is darker on its back than on its stomach. This is a protective arrangement which helps to camouflage it. In the Upside-down Catfish, this pattern is reversed and the stomach, which is held uppermost, becomes darker with the back lighter. It can, if it so desires, turn right side up and swim quite speedily in a most normal manner. Left undisturbed, it prefers to hide under an overhanging leaf or ledge, in the famous stomach-up position.

Family MONODACTYLIDAE

The deep, compressed silvery form of these fishes has given at least one, *Monodactylus argenteus,* the common name of Singapore Angel. In the trade it is also known as the Mono. There is no real relation to the Angelfish, genus *Pterophyllum,* however.

In nature, Monos are found in both fresh and salt water, from Malaya to East Africa. A fast moving, hardy fish, in nature it may reach a vertical length of ten inches. In the aquarium it prefers brackish water, is not a choosy feeder, prefers to school with others of its own kind, and is quite peaceful. Aquarium-raised specimens seldom exceed four inches. No sex distinctions are known.

Family POECILIIDAE

Those livebearers which are commonly kept as aquarium

Upside-down Catfish
Synodontis nigriventris
Photo by Dr. Herbert R. Axelrod

Mono
Monodactylus argenteus
Photo by A. Roth

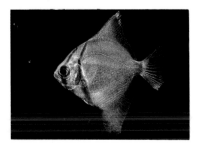

The unit shown can be used as both a breeding trap and also as a housing unit to hold the babies for a short while after they're born; it floats in the aquarium.

fishes are the Poeciliidae which range from southern United States to Central and South America. They are excellent community fishes, rarely belligerent and able to live under a varying range of conditions. If given a choice, however, they prefer to be kept in neutral to slightly alkaline water with the addition of a teaspoon of salt to every five gallons of aquarium water. While salt is harmful to aquarium plants in large quantities, this low level will not affect them and will be beneficial to most fishes.

Most livebearers lean heavily towards "vegetable" in their diets and will browse for hours on the algae growth in the aquarium. This is particularly true in the case of the mollies. However, they all, including the mollies, appreciate some live food and a varied diet.

Breeding Characteristics
Young livebearers all resemble females. It is only as they mature, usually between three and six months, that secondary sexual characteristics, which distinguish male from female, appear. These include such features as the high color of the guppy male and extended finnage, such as the large dorsal of the male sailfin molly and the sword of the male swordtail. During the early stages when these secondary characteristics first begin to appear, there is a noticeable change in the form of the anal fin. Rounded and fan-like in the juvenile livebearer, it begins to roll and forms the stick-like tube called the gonopodium, which is the organ used by the male livebearers for fertilization. Until this organ is fully developed, the young male is incapable of mating. Those breeders who are desirous of keeping their strains of fishes pure should bear in mind that the young male can mate once this organ has formed, even though the secondary characteristics, e.g., the sword of the swordtail, have not yet appeared. There are other features used to distinguish the male from the female livebearer. One is the so-called "gravid spot." This is a darkened area in the rear lower portion of the abdomen. Actually, this is not always accurate as a determinant

A breeder trap for livebearers. The babies fall to safety through the grid below the adult.

of sex. The gravid spot is actually the peritoneum, the sac-like membrane containing the internal organs. In later stages of pregnancy, because the developing young take up so much room in the abdominal cavity, this sac is pressed against the outer walls. However, in this author's opinion, the "gravid spot" is an inaccurate method of determining either the degree of pregnancy or even the very fact of pregnancy itself. Male livebearers which have eaten heavily frequently show this gravid spot and they certainly are not pregnant.

A more accurate method of determining the state of pregnancy is to view the female from above. Everyone is familiar with the normally streamlined shape of a fish. Pregnancy, especially in the later stages, interferes with this streamlining by causing a "side to side" bulge in the midsection. Experience will enable the aquarist to determine by the degree of the convexity the extent of pregnancy.

At present, we do not know definitely at how young an age a female livebearer can be fertilized. This is because it is possible for a female to store sperm within her body. This sperm remains viable for varying periods of time and thus is

available to fertilize the eggs which may develop later. Female guppies can give birth when three months old, while mollies and swordtails do not mature until six to eight months of age. The number of young may vary from as few as six or seven to several hundred.

It is recorded frequently in the scientific literature and popularly believed that the young livebearing fishes must manage to reach the surface and gulp a mouthful of air in order to actuate the mechanism of their swim bladders. However, many of the breeding traps which are designed to automatically segregate the young from their mother at birth are so constructed that the young cannot reach the surface. Nevertheless, somehow or other they do find a means to actuate their bladders and swim perfectly normally.

Guppy

Its correct Latin name is *Poecilia reticulata* although for many years the Guppy was known as *Lebistes reticulatus*. This latter name since then has been shown to have been given to the fish in error. The Guppy is probably the most popular of all the aquarium fishes and, in fact, the name "Guppy" (it rhymes with puppy) to many people is almost synonymous with tropical fishes.

Originating in Trinidad, several other nearby islands, and parts of northern South America, the guppy fitted all the essential requirements for achieving this popularity. It was small, peaceful, hardy, and in the early days of the aquarium hobby when the selection of fishes available was much smaller than it is today, the original male Guppy was considered a highly colored fish. The female was a drab gray. Today, through selective breeding, the size of the original Guppy has been doubled and, in some cases, almost tripled while the fins of the highly-bred Guppy have attained magnificent colors and proportions. Even the female today is coming into her own with some strains showing red, gold, blue, and black in certain body areas and particularly in the tail.

While not considered a saltwater fish, Guppies, by the gradual addition of salt to their aquarium, can be brought to a degree of tolerance at which they can exist and breed in a marine aquarium. This is practiced frequently by those hobbyists who

These Swordtails are very similar to wild-stock Xiphophorus helleri, *with a red-striped green body and numerous black spots. Photo by H. J. Richter.*

Blue Bicolor Delta Guppy
Poecilia reticulata
Photo by A. Roth

Purple Delta Guppy
Poecilia reticulata
Photo by A. Roth

A very nice specimen of the Marble Sailfin Molly, a form of Poecilia lati-pinna. *Photo by A. Roth.*

keep seahorses. Seahorses, which are marine fishes, will eat only live moving food. The young of those guppies kept and bred in the salt water tank provide a ready diet.

Mollies

The genus *Mollienesia,* from which the name *molly* was derived, has recently been vacated. So today, mollies in scientific nomenclature are known as *Poecilia* and are considered to be in the same genus as the guppy. For years it had been noticed that the guppy will, under certain circumstances, interbreed with the molly, and now the close relationship of the two has been confirmed.

There are three species of molly which are important to the aquarist. These are *Poecilia sphenops, Poecilia latipinna,* and *Poecilia velifera.* The latter two are known as the sailfin mollies, while the former is popularly called the sphenops molly. The name "sailfin" derives from the dorsal fin of the male which, developing as he matures, becomes greatly enlarged in adult specimens. Both *latipinna* and *velifera* are quite similar, the primary difference being the number of rays in the dorsal fin, *velifera* having eighteen whereas *latipinna* has only fourteen. In nature, both of these fishes are gray-green, although occasionally melanistic black specimens have been found.

The original sphenops molly, which is still popular with aquarists, is mottled black and silver. The posterior edge of the tail of the male is usually bordered with yellow or orange. The dorsal fin of the *sphenops* does not achieve the size of the sailfin dorsal. One easy way to distinguish *sphenops* from young

Black Sphenops Molly
Poecilia sphenops
Photo by A. Roth

Hybrid Sailfin Molly
Poecilia velifera X latipinna
Photo by A. Roth

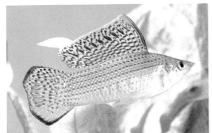

latipinna is by observing the placement of the dorsal. The dorsal of the *sphenops* molly originates behind the high point of the back, while the dorsal of the sailfin originates in front of the hump.

Most of the molly species have been interbred, resulting in many different color varieties and finnage shapes. To mention a few, we have solid black mollies, both sailfin type with an orange-bordered dorsal fin and *sphenops*. The latter is a very popular molly and usually has silver-rimmed eyes, whereas the sailfin molly's eyes are almost indistinguishable from the rest of the body because of their darkness. There are other black aquarium fishes, but none approach the soft, deep, velvety color of the molly. Albino forms, with red eyes, have also been developed, and a good specimen is magnificent. More recently, a molly has been developed with the outer rays of the tail elongated to form a lyre shape. The ventral fins are prolonged with tassels and it has a well-developed dorsal fin. The lyretails are available in black, the original gray-green, albino, and even a chocolate as well as an orange color. Mollies, like guppies, can be acclimated to full strength sea water. They also enjoy an algae growth in the aquarium on which they browse constantly. Lacking this, they should be provided either with a special molly food or occasional feeding of chopped boiled spinach.

Mollies are found from the southern United States down into Central America. They frequent both fresh and, in the coastal area, salt water. It is not unusual to find the sailfin molly, *Poecilia latipinna,* happily swimming and flaunting his magnificent dorsal

115

fin in the ocean off the Florida Keys.

Swordtails and Platies

There are three species in the genus *Xiphophorus* which are of special interest to aquarists. These are *Xiphophorus helleri, Xiphophorus variatus,* and *Xiphophorus maculatus.* The generic *Xiphophorus* means "sword bearer" and refers to the gonopodium. It does not refer to

Mickey Mouse Platy
Xiphophorus maculatus

Hi-fin Wagtail Platy
Xiphophorus maculatus

the swordlike extension of the lower rays of the tail of the *X. helleri.* Platies originally occupied a separate genus known as *Platypoecilus,* but in recent years studies have shown that the differences between *Xiphophorus* and *Platypoecilus* were not sufficient to warrant a separate genus. All platies and swordtails hybridize freely. As a result, many new and highly colored fishes have evolved, with a variety of fin formations.

In general, those hybrids in which the swordtail persists are called "swordtails" while the other are known simply as Platies. The platies themselves are further divided; the deeper-bodied being called *maculatus* Platies, while the slimmer platies are known as *variatus.* The original *X. variatus* was a blue fish with a red tail and a yellow or orange dorsal fin. A yellow-tail variety was also found in nature and these two were known individually as Redtail Variatus and Yellowtail Variatus. Today, the Yellowtail is seldom seen, but the Redtail with its shimmering blue body is still popular and is known simply as Platy Variatus. Through crossings with other types of platies and swordtails they have developed such color varieties as the following:

Sunset Variatus — this has a yellow, almost sweet potato colored body with an orange tail.

Marigold Variatus — similar to the sunset, from which it was developed, with a bright orange body. The males in particular are extremely colorful.

Black Variatus — the body is black with a yellow or colorless tail.

Tuxedo Variatus — similar to the black variatus but the head and throat are yellow.

Redtail Black Variatus — this fish has a black body with a red tail and a yellow dorsal.

White Variatus — the body is ivory with a red tail and yellow dorsal fin.

Albino Variatus — this is a fairly recent development. It is similar to the white variatus but as is characteristic of albinos, the eyes are red.

In addition to the various color varieties, a "hi-fin" variatus has been developed. This is an extremely attractive fish. It is similar in coloration to the other varieties of variatus, but the dorsal fin of the male has been broadened and elongated.

Platy Maculatus — the original *X. maculatus* was a dull colored fish with a few black spots. Hybridization with the *X. helleri* resulted in the early color varieties of platies. The development of the color varieties in the variatus did not take place until the late 1940's and 50's, whereas colorful maculatus platies were produced in the 30's.

Wag platies — the term "wag" refers to the fact that the fins, particularly the dorsal and the

Two strains of the Platy X. maculatus. **Top:** *Bleeding Heart Platy. Photo by A. van den Nieuwenhuizen.* **Bottom:** *Painted Platies. Photo by M. Gilroy.*

Top: An extraordinary Hi-fin Variatus Platy, with its fanlike dorsal reaching beyond the end of the tail. Photo by R. Zukal. *Bottom:* A Gold Flame Twinbar Swordtail, a fairly new strain. Photo by Dr. H. Grier.

caudal, are black. For example, a red Platy with black fins would be called a Red Wag Platy, a gold Platy with black fins would be called a Gold Wag Platy, and so on. A black Platy with colorless fins which is known simply as a Black Platy would be called a Black Wag if the fins were dark.

Moon Platies — early platies had a dominant characteristic called "the moon" which was simply a crescent-shaped black marking on the caudal peduncle, which is the base of the body on which the tail is set. In fact, an early name for the Platy was moon, or moonfish. This factor has been largely bred out, but it still persists in certain color varieties, notably the Gold Crescent, Red Crescent, and Blue

Crescent, which are solid colored fishes except for this marking.

In addition, there is Tuxedo Maculatus. The tuxedo marking is a darkened area of the body beginning approximately at the gill cover and extending to the tail. The head, neck and throat can be any one of a number of colors, and the fins usually are colorless. For example, the red tuxedo would have the forward portion red and the rear half black. If the fins were also dark the fish would be known as a red tuxedo wag platy.

Xiphophorus helleri — the original color variety of the helleri or, as it is more popularly known, the Swordtail, was predominantly green with a red stripe along the caudal fin. The swordlike extension of the lower rays of the tail was usually yellow lined with black; altogether a graceful, hardy and extremely attractive fish. Two judicious crossings with the above resulted in first, the brick red sword, which is an orange-red fish with a pattern of lines on its body, and the velvet red sword, a bright solid red-colored fish. In addition to green, red, gold, and black Swordtails we have the tuxedo and wag pattern developed in the swordtail in the various color varieties. One popular variety is the albino, which is a clear gold with a red eye.

There is no doubt that as time goes on you will see many more new and colorful varieties of platies and swordtails being developed. Peaceful, hardy, and attractive, the swordtails make ideal aquarium fishes. At times, the male swordtail has been accused of being a bully. It has been said that an adult male swordtail would not tolerate another male in his territory. However, this problem can be

Xiphophorus helleri

Xiphophorus helleri

Xiphophorus helleri X maculatus

Xiphophorus helleri

The elegant but somewhat delicate Glass Catfish, Kryptopterus bicirrhis.

avoided by having a number of male swordtails in the aquarium rather than two or three, provided an adequate number of females are present, of course.

One word of caution — swordtails are notorious jumpers, so make sure that the aquarium is well covered.

Family SILURIDAE

These are all Old World catfishes, only one of which particularly interests the aquarist. This is *Kryptopterus bicirrhis,* the Glass Catfish. This unusual catfish from India and the Greater Sunda Islands reaches a length of almost four inches in the aquarium. The unique feature is the translucence of its knife-shaped body. The ribs and sac enclosing its internal organs are clearly visible when a light is held behind it. There are two large feelers extending from the head. This is a schooling type of fish and one of the few catfishes which does not inhabit the bottom area. Rather, it hovers in mid-aquarium, the body moving with a wavelike motion characteristic of the species. The Glass Catfish does not take kindly to dry foods, and if it is to be kept in good health it must have an ample supply of live food which it eats gluttonously, the stomach sometimes blowing up to the size and shape of a marble. At times, when fed heavily, the Glass Catfish ingests so much that it seems impossible for him to survive, but apparently it does no harm as he is back again at the next feeding, darting rapidly in to seize his share.

The Last Word!

Faced with the vast array and variety in the dealer's tanks the beginner tends to become very enthusiastic when choosing fish. At times he lets this enthusiasm carry him away, and as a result he overstocks.

At first, it is much better to introduce just a few fish to the newly set-up tank after allowing it to settle for at least a week to show up any weaknesses or malfunction of equipment.

Don't overstock at any cost.

Suggested Reading

The following books published by T.F.H. Publications are available at pet shops and book stores everywhere.

GENERAL AQUARIUM HANDBOOKS AND FISH CATALOGS

All About Aquariums
By Earl Schneider
ISBN 0-87666-768-X
T.F.H. PS-601
A very complete general introduction to the beginning aquarists or those just thinking about it. Excellent for pre-planning as you consider your options in setting up.

Aquarium Keeping...Easy as ABC
By Werner Weiss
ISBN 0-87666-100-X
T.F.H. PS-831
A beautiful large-format beginner's book that includes everything one needs to know to enter the "art" of fishkeeping—plenty about the tanks and the fishes too!

How to Keep and Breed Tropical Fish
By Dr. C. W. Emmens
ISBN 0-87666-499-0
T.F.H. H-910
Practical answers to the typical problems faced by beginning hobbyists, including breeding, feeding, and disease, as well as basic setup and maintenance.

Starting Your Tropical Aquarium
By Dr. Herbert R. Axelrod
ISBN 0-86622-105-0
T.F.H. PS-840
Contains a wealth of valuable information not found in many other beginner's books, including a chapter on fish genetics and another on the naming of the cardinal tetra.

Vierke's Aquarium Book
By Jörg Vierke
ISBN 0-86622-103-4
T.F.H. PS-834
One of Germany's leading aquarists presents one of the most thorough aquarium books ever written, discussing virtually every aspect of aquarium keeping—much more than just fishes. Equipment, plants, breeding, feeding, and raising fishes are discussed in elaborate detail.

Exotic Tropical Fishes Expanded Edition
By Dr. Herbert R. Axelrod, Dr. C. W. Emmens, Dr. Warren E. Burgess, and Neal Pronek.
ISBN 0-87666-543-1 (hardcover),
ISBN 0-87666-537-7 (looseleaf)
T.F.H. H-1028 (hardcover),
H-1028L (looseleaf)
The "bible" of freshwater ornamental fishes—contains comprehensive information on aquarium maintenance, plants, and commercial culture, as well as over 1,000 color photos and entries on many hundreds of species. New supplements are issued every month in *Tropical Fish Hobbyist* magazine, and may be placed into the looseleaf edition.

Dr. Axelrod's Atlas of Freshwater Aquarium Fishes
By Dr. Herbert R. Axelrod, Dr. Warren E. Burgess, Neal Pronek, and Jerry G. Walls.

ISBN 0-86622-052-6
T.F.H. H-1077
The ultimate aquarium book—
illustrated with over 4000 color
photos. Almost every fish available
to hobbyists is illustrated! Species
are grouped geographically and by
family for easy reference. No
aquarist's library is complete
without it!

SPECIALIZED AQUARIUM TOPICS

Aquarium Plants
By Dr. Karel Rataj and T. J.
Horeman
ISBN 0-87666-455-9
T.F.H. H-966
The most complete volume ever
published about aquarium plants, it
includes taxonomic information as
well as ecology, reproduction and
cultivation, and guides to proper
aquarium lighting.

Diseases of Aquarium Fishes
By Dr. Robert J. Goldstein
ISBN 0-87666-795-7
T.F.H. PS-201
A discussion of many of the
parasites most likely to be
encountered by the aquarist, with
suggestions on effective treatment.

Textbook of Fish Health
By Dr. George Post
ISBN 0-87666-599-7
T.F.H. H-1043
This volume not only covers the
identification and treatment of fish
diseases, but gives special
attention to mechanisms and
causes of infection—valuable aids
to prevention.

SPECIALIZED FISH BOOKS

*African Cichlids of Lakes Malawi
and Tanganyika*
By Dr. Herbert R. Axelrod and Dr.
Warren E. Burgess

ISBN 0-87666-792-2
T.F.H. PS-703
The standard reference to one of
the most popular groups of fishes
in the hobby, with complete
information on care and
maintenance, but most importantly,
with over 450 color photos to aid
the hobbyist in easy identification
of Rift Lake cichlids.

All About Guppies
By Dr. Leon F. Whitney and Paul
Hahnel
ISBN 0-87666-083-9
T.F.H. PS-603
The breeding and raising of
guppies, including anatomy,
feeding, heredity, disease, and
breeding programs.

Angelfish
By Braz Walker
ISBN 0-87666-755-8
T.F.H. PS-711
Covers all important aspects of
keeping and breeding the
freshwater angelfishes.

Handbook of Discus
By Jack Wattley
ISBN 0-86622-037-2
T.F.H. H-1070
A comprehensive guide to discus
husbandry by the field leader.
Contains absolutely everything you
need to know to sucessfully raise
the king of freshwater fishes—the
discus.

Koi of the World
By Dr. Herbert R. Axelrod
ISBN 0-87666-092-8
T.F.H. H-947
A spectacularly beautiful book
loaded with full-color photos of
many different varieties of koi. Of
great value in identification of the
many color and scale patterns of
koi available.

Index

Aquarium keeping is a family hobby. It appeals to all members of the family. Over 20,000,000 people in the U.S. keep fishes; England boasts 11,000,000 while Australia and Canada claim 1,000,000 hobbyists each. Specialized aquarium stores sell everything necessary for a successful aquarium.

CO-003

A COMPLETE INTRODUCTION TO

SETTING UP AN AQUARIUM

Cichlasoma festae, *the so-called "red terror," is a mean fish, but its bright hues represent one of primary attractions of tropical fishes— color! Photo by Rainer Stawikowski.*